MW01593752

In Whatever State I Am
Learning the Lessons of Contentment

by Lee Hotchkiss

Edited by Chuck Peters
Cover Design & Page Layout by Chris Gates

Books may be ordered through
www.leehotchkiss.com

Printed in the USA by Snowfall Press

Table of Contents

Acknowledgments

Those who attempt putting ideas on a page know how doubts creep in along the way as a normal part of the writing process. It is risky business. It demands that we let others peek into private areas of our lives as they critique our work and opinions. The extent to which we bare our souls and tell our stories generates and exposes vulnerability. Those who honestly and graciously give feedback are as valuable as gold and silver.

Singling out some to thank is risky too, lest I forget anyone, but let me mention a few who read early drafts and made comments which God used to encourage me to proceed.

Thank you Bill and Thelma for asking your small group to read and discuss the content while it was still coming together and in need of a rewrite. Thank you Bob and Elaine, Chuck and Karin, Jerry and Shari, Jim and Sharon, Fran, Dina and Margie for your encouragement and suggestions.

Thanks to friends Joe and Toni, Dudley and Inge, who read the manuscript and gave feedback from the perspective of reading together and discussing the content as couples.

Family support was pivotal. Thanks Chuck for lending me your editing talent for this project. Cris for letting him moonlight, and Tim and Sue for sending helpful ideas.

Lastly, thank you John for letting us park our RV on your property in sunny California where ideas had time to percolate. What a delightful spot.

~ Lee

Dedicated to my wife Beverly, my life partner and fellow traveler on the journey, who has been graciously faster than me at learning the lessons of contentment.

Introduction

The subject of contentment is exceedingly relevant today. Never have we had so much, and been so busy in the pursuit of our dreams but generally felt so discontent. Genuine contentment is elusive. We live at a time in history that is filled with an endless stream of empty promises and formulas for happiness. Like so many mirages on a hot dry desert road, they disappear as we get closer. Contemporary society promises much but delivers little real contentment.

There are a growing number in the contemporary church preaching confusing messages about the secrets of success and gaining wealth as if that will provide contentment. Christian leaders are often better known for their drivenness and success in building large ministries than for modeling personal contentment. The believing community needs a call back to its roots. I do not suggest a return to a simpler time or a retreat to a quieter rural life style. We cannot create a world of idealism and nostalgia out of romantic ideas from the past. We also underestimate the challenge if we frame the solution as merely simplifying life or lowering expectations (even though both activities may be helpful).

The command to be content in Scripture is simple and straightforward. "Keep your lives free from the love of money and be content with what you have" but the writer quickly adds the promise of God's presence which makes obedience possible, "because God has said, 'Never will I leave you; never will I forsake you'" (Hebrews 13:5).

We must be willing to explore the foundations of our faith, returning to the truth of the Scriptures that transcend time and place. It is here, I believe, we will find the lessons that will teach us how we may experience the contentment that God has for us. The answers are found in learning to live God-centered lives in his presence as we honestly and consistently apply his word to daily life.

Often we learn best from and with others. I share observations and snapshots from my personal journey to illustrate how God has shown his faithfulness. My prayer is that you will develop a growing trust to share experiences of struggles and triumphs (your personal reflections) with your spouse, study partner, class or small group using the questions at the end of each chapter that are provided to help get dialogue and discussion started. I trust that God will stir your heart, possibly convict, hopefully encourage and certainly bless you as you read, discuss and explore these very personal lessons on contentment.

Chapter 1

Fantasies of the Open Road and Other Distant Horizons

"May the words of my mouth and the meditation of my heart be pleasing in your sight, O LORD, my Rock and my Redeemer." Psalm 19:14

My mind runs in high gear as the sun finally shows itself over the horizon. The early twilight gives way to dawn and transforms the desert hills in the distance. I feel the warmth of the rising sun and expectancy of a new day as the golden glow gently warms through the windshield and quickly erases the chill left from the crisp night air. What were only twinkling lights in the distance begin to take on identifiable shapes of truck stops and motels. The high desert plains have now replaced the gently rolling prairies as the mid-west turns into the magnificent West, the big sky country. I love the open-road early in the morning before the traffic builds on the interstate. It is breathtakingly beautiful. No matter how many times I drive it, I find that my pulse quickens with anticipation of the dry air, open spaces and stark beauty of the West. It stirs my imagination and my fantasies.

At moments like this, alone with my thoughts on the open road, one can almost hear the "meditations of the heart" speaking out loud. Escape fantasies and daydreams emerge from their hiding places and whisper their tantalizing promises of some future imagined contentment. The new vistas and images stimulate thoughts of new beginnings that promise to leave old problems behind. Each person develops the mental storyline with unique features but we all indulge to some degree in the mental exploration that some distant horizon might be more idyllic.

One of the fun things I like to do on these long-haul drives is to imagine what it would be like to live in these places. What would life be like here? Where's the closest home improvement store and convenience grocery? Where would I build a house to take advantage of this spectacular view? Would a garden grow in this climate? A log cabin would really fit nicely in that canyon or up on that ridge. I wonder if there are fish in that lake. Daydreaming spices up any road trip and helps pass the time while sleepy passengers doze. One can envision stepping back in time and contemplating the life experiences of those who traveled this way in covered wagons and on horseback moving only a few hard miles a day. What must it have been like for those early pioneers to watch a thunderstorm roll across an open sky and smell the freshness of a summer rain while exposed to the elements? What went through their minds as they traveled so slowly day after day? What dreams did they have? What secret thoughts of future contentment helped them pass the time and endure the drudgery and dust of the trail?

Sometimes I sit at home and look at road maps and imagine trips. I run my finger over the crooked lines that track from state to state picturing in my mind familiar places that flash back into view from memory and wonder about places I've never been. My father-in-law did this same kind of trip planning in his mind and found great pleasure indulging in fantasy travel to interesting places. I wonder how many others do this kind of adventure travel planning.

These fantasy rituals stem from the idea that life may be better somewhere else. Not that it is so terribly bad where I am, but maybe somewhere else or something different might be more exciting and bring me more contentment. Maybe I am missing out by being here instead of there. Would a change of place or circumstances cause me to be more content? What are some of the things that you daydream about? What triggers your imagination and fantasies? Would a promotion at work make you content? How much difference would a new toy or possession really make? Is your view of contentment contingent upon the behavior of another person?

What do the meditations of your heart tell you about your value system? Do they provide a window of insight into what you believe holds the promise of greater happiness and contentment? Acknowledging and clarifying these thoughts can be insightful, but can also be a little intimidating. Learning to live a more God-centered life can start with taking a few awkward steps of self disclosure.

David prayed that God would be pleased with both the words he spoke and the secret inner meditations of his heart (Psalm 19:14). This is a great place to begin. It's not easy for some of us to take the risk and openly share these private inner thoughts. It can, however, shed valuable light on our beliefs about contentment when we begin to put these daydreams into words. Ask God to guide you in the words you share with others while exploring this subject.

Discontentment is the opposite of contentment. Just as daydreams and fantasies provide a window into the soul, so do our words of discontentment, complaint and criticism.

I must confess that I am not always content. As I look back over my life there have been periods when I have been negative, and played the role of the critic with the polished skills of a veteran fault-finder. There is something fundamentally appealing about being a critic; it strokes the ego by elevating oneself to the status of expert. It feels good and bad at the same time. It leads to pride, leaves a nasty aftertaste in the soul and scuttles any hope of finding genuine contentment.

Our culture today is loaded with opportunities to practice being a malcontent. It is politically correct to be unhappy and angry about something. Displaying an angry edge of discontentment is definitely "in." The political party not in power criticizes those in office. Then a few years later they reverse roles. The trend in cable news is toward less news and more commentary, less factual reporting and more opinion of guests who often angrily argue their entrenched viewpoints. Producers invite a conservative and liberal, then throw out loaded questions like red meat to a pack of hungry wild animals and watch the verbal fight. Rather than expanding solid journalistic coverage, we have a proliferation of news-entertainment shows that use thinly veiled sarcasm, ridicule and angry people shouting at each other, usually simultaneously. Rather than becoming better informed on a subject, we are overexposed to sound bites and video clips that run in endless loops cleverly chosen to manipulate us and to support the perspective of the host. Ranting and out of control emotional meltdowns may make for good television ratings, but I fear it is feeding a spirit of hopelessness and simmering populist rage in our nation. All of this can erode a spirit of contentment.

I confess that I often take the bait too quickly and find it difficult to break free from the hold of the cynical and avoid its effects on my spirit. My wife, Bev, says "Just don't watch." But as a recovering news junkie who is intensely interested in the world around me, shutting out the stimulation of cable news is easier said than done. I justify my actions with the need to keep up with what is happening in the world.

Of course she is right. Setting good boundaries on amount and selection of media intake is a good idea. I can't blame television; it only takes advantage of what is already in my heart. The comments of the media's talking heads only fan the flame of my discontentment that is eager to respond. I am, however, not just a responder programmed to react. I have a responsibility to learn how to set the pace of my spirit and manage it to the glory of God. I must learn to be a more consistent initiator of that which produces a right spirit.

God's peace and rest are available and he has promised to complete the work that he has started in me (Philippians 1:6). Many times experiencing greater contentment means learning new ways while resisting the old. It may require some serious change, adding new skills and learning to think differently if we are to successfully go against the strong current of our society.

Contentment is learned. The Apostle Paul said, "I have learned to be content whatever the circumstances" (Philippians 4:11, NIV) or "I have learned in whatever state I am, to be content" (NKJV). That is a pretty bold statement. I wish I could say that it was true of me. What I can honestly say is that I am learning (present tense) the lessons of contentment. Some days I see more progress than others. But there is progress and that gives me hope.

Lesson one: Contentment can be learned. God is at work and he is the master teacher.

How did Paul learn what he called the "secret of being content" (Philippians 4:12) and what was his learning curve? How did he change from being a critic and harsh persecutor of the church to being content while experiencing the hardships of missionary conditions? Did he ever experience regression or have setbacks? Did the evil twins of greed and coveting ever sneak back into Paul's life to rob him of his contentment? Did he ever battle with desires that grew out of what he saw and experienced as he sat under house arrest waiting for trial? How did he guard himself in the battle against, what the book of Proverbs describes as the insatiable desire of the eyes? "Death and Destruction are never satisfied, and neither are the eyes of man" (Proverbs 27:20). If this verse is describing what is universally true of the human experience, how did Paul personally deal with its reality? How did he protect himself from a spirit of entitlement? I wish that I could interview Paul and ask him some tough questions. How did he keep from judging others and not allow his spirit to slip into envy and jealousy? I am thankful for the personal insights that he shared, but I long for more detail of his journey. We do, however, have a trustworthy word from the Holy Spirit who was at work in Paul's life and is still at work today in your life and mine. As we examine the Scriptures we begin to discover that there is ample material upon which to draw for learning the key lessons of contentment.

Reflection Questions and Small Group Activities:

1. Have you ever dreamed of hitting the road and exploring new places? What makes the idea sound attractive? What other contentment fantasies do you entertain?

2. List the top five escape (contentment) fantasies common to your age group.

3. What changes in public national spirit have you observed? How have expressions of discontentment increased? List three cable news shows that are the most argumentative.

4. Discuss how this culture of discontent affects you personally.

5. Are there any areas where you need to set limits or boundaries to protect your spirit?

6. Does anyone come to mind who you think models contentment? What stands out in their life?

7. How confident are you that God can teach you to be content?

Prayer:

Lord, we confess that we are frequently not content. We too quickly think of running away rather than honestly facing the areas where we need to grow. We are too often carried along with the current of our times taking on the hopelessness and cynicism of those around us rather than becoming transformed into lights that shine in dark places. Thank you for the promise that you are at work in us. Teach us the lessons of contentment. Forgive us for being resistant to your leadership in our lives as the master teacher and Sovereign Lord of our circumstances. Help us learn from each other and pray for each other as we share our stories and struggles. "May the words of my mouth and the meditation of my heart be pleasing in your sight, O LORD, our Rock and our Redeemer." In Jesus' name, amen.

Chapter 2

The Campground

"You shall not covet your neighbor's house" Exodus 20:17

Today is a special day. Bev and I are sitting quietly in the beautiful Sierra Nevada Mountains of northern California. It is our first day of rest and reflection of what we hope will be about six months of sabbatical. We've never done this before – stopped to smell the roses for a significant period of time. After more than 40 busy years of marriage and ministry we have decided to take time to watch the pines and redwoods grow, sleep in, breathe a little fresh air and spend some quality time with our grandchildren. Bev plans to catch up on her Sudoku books and I have some writing projects I would like to tackle.

The campground is quiet this morning with a gentle mountain breeze moving the air in and out of our recently acquired used motor home. I hear the rhythmic pulse of a sprinkler watering the newly cut grass nearby. It smells fresh and clean. The RV Park is well kept and populated with a mix of working and retired people, serious travelers known as "full-timers" and weekenders up from the valley for a respite to beat the heat. It's not hard to tell the groups apart. The working people stay in the more permanent sites at the back of the park, live in smaller trailers or fifth wheels and leave early each morning for road construction jobs or work in the sawmill directly behind the park (Oh, the sweet smell of pines and freshly sawn lumber) or in what's left of the logging industry. The retirees sleep late; they tend to be traveling in large luxurious motor homes or new fifth wheel trailers with multiple slide-outs pulled by big pickup trucks. They engage in small talk about traveling, the price of gas, the advantages of diesel pushers, and other trivia. They spend time washing bugs off their big windshields, walking their dogs and "eye balling" the other vehicles. The RV world provides a wonderful platform to create and express personal identity and consumer society is clearly on display. These vehicles can truly become extensions of one's persona.

We have been learning as newcomers, trying to blend in and figure out how things work. We are beginning to have stories to tell about blown tires, the best wax for fiberglass and gas mileage. We now have 3,400 miles under our belts and are beginning to feel less like outsiders. We bought our 1991 Fleetwood Bounder online and drove across the states from Florida.

Bev spent most of the morning cleaning and washing all the windows both inside and out. She is most content when she is busy serving, cleaning, or as she likes to say "feathering her nest." As she finishes her chores, a neighbor from a big new motor home stops by to say hello, commenting on how nice our motor home looks. This is polite, but seems a bit odd as ours is without doubt the oldest among the traveling retired group. It stands out as a bit "vintage," due to its 17 years and 127,000 miles of use. But as we talk it becomes clear that she is sincere and eager to make friends. Before long we are on a tour of her beautiful new 37-foot motor home with three slide-outs, leather chairs, two flat screen HDTVs and all the bells and whistles that come with a top of the line rig. We have a delightful time talking about all kinds of things. She seems a little lonely as her husband is still actively working as CEO of a nearby hospital. They own a home a few miles away and don't really fit neatly into any of the social groups in the park. It is a good reminder that contentment is not just about possessions but also about relationships.

We return from our tour of the big luxurious motor home next door and I immediately go online to find out how much it cost. Wow! I had no idea how much you could spend. After indulging in some ostensibly harmless, but never-the-less spiritually questionable mental fantasy comparison window-shopping, my prayer over lunch is simple and straightforward; Thank you Lord for what you have provided. Help me to not covet the big and beautiful travel homes that belong to others. Help me to be content with what I have.

I have learned from experience that if I am not careful to cultivate a thankful heart and nip covetousness in the bud I will get sucked into the vortex of the comparison game. I quickly lose appreciation for what I have and begin to look with distain upon that which is not the latest style or that which has a little rust and wear around the edges, even if it does function just fine. I am amazed by how easily my ego begins to make these comparisons and how quickly my contentment factor fades. A spirit of coveting is only a glance away.

Coveting needs to be acknowledged for what it is, breaking the tenth commandment, "You shall not covet your neighbor's house" (Exodus 20:17). The Bible clearly calls it sin and any sin contaminates, deadens and ensnares the soul. It is also offensive to God. The Spirit of God uses the Law to expose a heart of discontent for what God has graciously provided. He patiently and repeatedly teaches this lesson in learning contentment.

Lesson one: Contentment can be learned. God is at work and he is the master teacher.

Lesson two: Coveting is off limits.

Coveting can come in many subtle forms. We can covet the position someone has in an organization, the husband or wife of another, the financial blessing or ministry success that someone enjoys, a classic car or a prized piece of antique furniture. When God convicts of any sin, including the sin of coveting, we are called to humbly confess and turn away from it in a spirit of repentance. God's grace is sufficient to cleanse our hearts from coveting and enable the ugly habit to be broken. "If we confess our sins, he is faithful and just and will forgive us our sins and purify us from all unrighteousness" (1 John 1:9).

It is possible to be carried along with the swift current of the materialism of the day and become callous and blind to the sensitivity to the Spirit's gentle rebuke. Peter described the characteristics of the false teachers of his day when he said, "they are experts in greed" (2 Peter 2:14). This phrase can also be translated, "they have hearts trained in greed."

Some penetrating and possibly revealing questions might include: Have you trained your heart in greed to the extent that you have lost spiritual sensitivity to the deadening effects of coveting? Have you honed your skills in making comparisons so that the resulting climate of criticism and coveting seem quite normal? Has your expertise at rationalizing and excusing yourself from the convicting truth of the tenth commandment deadened your awareness of the spiritual reality of your condition? Like the proverbial frog in the kettle, have you grown accustomed to the rising temperature of the water around you that you are oblivious to the changes taking place?

Financial commentators and pundits often say that the stock market is driven by fear and greed. A few years ago a quote from the 1987 movie Wall Street, became famous in which the character Gordon Gekko boldly stated, "greed, for lack of a better word, is good. Greed is right, greed works."[1] Popular culture attempts to put a positive spin on greed and tries to pass it off as harmless or even as positive motivation. The serious follower of Jesus Christ, however, who desires to learn contentment must see through this deception and keep a sharp eye out for greed's dangerous and deadening affects on the soul. The New Testament uses a cluster of words to speak about this spiritual danger: coveting, desire, lust and greed. A short selection of verses is listed on the next page. Take the time to read these Scriptures. It is a spiritual exercise that is well worth the effort. Notice the frequency and extent to which Jesus and the Apostles draw attention to, and warn of, the spiritual implications of unchecked desires.

None of us are beyond greed's seductive grasp. I recommend that you pause here to read and meditate on the sixteen verses of Matthew 6:19-34 found in the Sermon on the Mount. Note how Jesus connects the issues of fear and greed. This passage serves as an excellent introduction into a study of the topic of greed and its relationship to contentment.

1

    Wall Street, the movie written by Oliver Stone and Stanley Weiser, released 1987, quote from The Internet Movie Database http://www.imdb.com/title/tt0094291/quotes

A selected list of New Testament passages using the words coveting, desire, lust and greed; Mark 7:22, Luke 12:15, Acts 20:33, Romans 1:29, 7:7-8, 13:14, 1 Corinthians 5:9-11, 6:9-10, 10:6-7, Galatians 5:16-17, 24, Ephesians 2:3, 4:19, 5:5, Colossians 3:5-6, 1 Thessalonians 2:5, 1 Timothy 6:9, James 4:2, 2 Peter 2:14

Reflection Questions and Small Group Activities:

1. In what areas of life are you most susceptible to making comparisons?

2. What practical steps can you take to guard against greed?

3. When was the last time you felt convicted about coveting?

4. Where do you tend to look for contentment? Poll your small group.

a) relationships

b) acquiring things

c) accomplishing tasks

5. Come up with other examples in the media where greed or coveting is portrayed as good.

6. Which of the Scripture passages on greed stood out to you?

7. Discuss how your small group can change the way you talk socially about your possessions so that it doesn't lead to bragging or "one-upmanship?"

Prayer:

Dear Lord, thank you for providing for our needs. Help us to distinguish between our needs and our wants. Forgive us for too often crossing the line into sin's territory of greed and coveting. Teach us to rest in the green pastures of your provision, content, refreshed and restored beside the quiet waters that truly satisfy. Teach us to wait upon you and drink from the streams of living water. In Jesus' name, amen.

Chapter 3

Tests

"And my God will meet all your needs according to his glorious riches in Christ Jesus." Philippians 4:19

"Did you hear that loud bang?" I asked Bev. I could tell by the look on her face that she had. "We'd better pull off and take a look." We had just blown a tire on the motor home. We were traveling from Florida to Illinois soon after our purchase and were still getting acquainted with how everything worked. As we surveyed the situation we realized that we had limited tools, no jack and a six inch gash on an inside rear dual tire. What we thought would be solved by a quick call to the auto club turned into a two hour wait beside the freeway and a hopeful dialogue that maybe someone could be sent from Indiana to our location in central Illinois. After all it was a weekend.

Sometimes tests force us to exercise ingenuity and creativity. As we waited, it crossed my mind that if we were on a remote road in Alaska I would have to figure this out on my own. We experimented with putting various size blocks under the hydraulic levelers to lift the wheels (they are not designed for changing tires). Scavenged kitchen utensils allowed us to remove the air fill extenders and chrome lug covers. Eventually we found a tire iron and were able to get the big duals off and the spare back on. It was with a good deal of contentment that we called the auto club back to cancel our request for help. They were happy and so were we.

Successful accomplishment provides a surge of contentment even if short lived.

The good feelings lasted about a hundred miles until again – Bang! The companion dually blew and we had to repeat the process. It was much easier the second time. I was learning that tires can look good, show no weather checking, and have lots of tread but be damaged from sitting parked too long with weight on them. We also learned that big truck tires are expensive and can come in unusual sizes that are hard to find.

Tests, like tires, can come in many sizes, shapes and forms, but they are all generally unpleasant. During my years in school I never liked tests. I knew that tests were designed to show what I had learned but I always feared that they would expose what I had failed to learn. Later I discovered that most people experience some degree of what my counseling professor called test anxiety. Tests are pretty much universally distasteful experiences.

I wonder if Abraham experienced anxiety when, we are told, "God tested him" (Genesis 22:1, Hebrews 11:17). I have no doubt that God knew, before it occurred, what the outcome would be. In the bigger context of the unfolding flow of salvation history it makes sense that this event was part of what God was revealing and demonstrating about what would later become known as the story of redemption. In the New Testament, Abraham's faith is used as the model for personal saving faith. "Abraham believed God, and it was credited to him as righteousness" (Romans 4:3). God had made a covenant promise and Abraham believed him. His act of obedience clearly shows Abraham's belief in the Sovereign Almighty God who had revealed himself. God had promised to supply that which Abraham could not. Unlike the flat tire there is nothing that we can do to save ourselves. God has provided salvation through Jesus Christ's substitutionary work of atonement accomplished on the cross. At the core of a true relationship with God is a heart that takes God at his word. Faith is waiting with a sense of expectancy to see how he will faithfully do what he has promised. This delights God.

We cannot be certain to what extent Abraham understood the prophetic significance of his answer to Isaac's question about not having a lamb to sacrifice. "God himself will provide the lamb for the burnt offering, my son" (Genesis 22:8). This statement is charged with meaning for us as we look back over time and see the event in context of what God had planned. John understood the connection when he said of Jesus, "Look, the Lamb of God, who takes away the sin of the world!" (John 1:29). God has provided for our greatest need, the need for cleansing from sin and the need for right standing before a Holy God by supplying his Son as the sacrificial Lamb. As the Apostle Paul wrote so clearly, "But now a righteousness from God, apart from law, has been made known, to which the Law and the Prophets testify. This righteousness from God comes through faith in Jesus Christ to all who believe" (Romans 3:21-22).

Paul continued to stress the universality of the human need with his blanket indictment, "all have sinned and fall short of the glory of God" (Romans 3:23). Then he laid out the sufficiency of God's provision for man's sin in the atoning sacrifice of Jesus Christ. He pointed to Christ's death as the only possible solution to provide for justice to be done, for God's wrath to be turned away, and for our redemption to be carried out. God has provided for our greatest need – to be made alive in Jesus Christ (vv. 24-26).

In addition to his provision for the work of salvation, God is also presiding over a process of transformation. He is at work conforming the believer into the image of his Son Jesus Christ, from glory to glory (2 Corinthians 3:18). Even though we may be more preoccupied about getting the car fixed, the rent paid or who is going to win the next election, God is at work in changing us. He patiently exposes what is in our heart and faithfully deals with what is inconsistent with the perfection of his Son Jesus. He has promised to complete this work of transformation, even though it is still very much in process (Philippians 1:6). It will be glorious to behold when he unveils the finished product. It will be worth it all, including the tests.

The New Testament writers help us understand not only what God is doing, but some idea of how he is doing it (James 1:3-4, 1 Peter 1:3-7). We are told by Peter that God uses "all kinds of trials" to demonstrate the genuineness of our faith. James adds that "the testing of your faith," through these unpleasant experiences, produces maturity and makes us complete. The way to exercise faith, in light of this truth, is to practice the instruction of James, "Consider it pure joy…whenever you face trials of many kinds" (James 1:2).

Today was another one of those "test" kind of days for Bev and me. My journal would read:

> The stock market had another major drop. The news is filled with stories of banks and other Wall Street firms in trouble and there is a lot of talk and no little fear of an economic collapse in the credit markets. The financial markets world-wide are being shaken. Our retirement nest egg is shrinking day by day (up to 50% along with everyone else's) and there is a real temptation to respond with fear and anger. My doctor

and hospital bills keep growing, now somewhere around $190,000 and today we discovered that the health insurance company will not cover any of my cardiac rehab. It makes us wonder how much of the other bills they will reject. (At the time of writing I am three weeks into recovery from a quintuple by-pass heart surgery.) Our idyllic sabbatical living in the motor home has been suddenly interrupted. A few days ago, when we weren't sure what to put down as our permanent address, a hospital employee jokingly said, "We have treated a number of homeless people before." Even though this was said in humor, it was nonetheless a little embarrassing. It was one of those moments of pause when one is tempted to question, what is going on and what are we doing? In the midst of all this I tell Bev that I feel a deep sense of peace that God would provide. She agreed.

God did provide. All of the medical bills were paid through several different sources. The recovery in the motor home went well. I slept the first several weeks in a lawn lounge-recliner chair with a piece of memory foam on top that fit snuggly in the aisle of the main cabin just behind the driver's seat. We also enjoyed a nice break from the confined space provided by the generosity of friends who took a vacation and asked us to house sit while they were away. Another friend, a physical therapist, came and gave me pointers and instruction on how to do my own rehab program. God supplied all that we needed.

I am (like many people) sometimes prone to anxiety. But I can honestly say that I felt enveloped by God's peace. I know that we had hundreds of friends praying for us during that time and it reminded me that God's peace is a gift of his grace.

Contentment is an element of God's peace. Contentment is a gift of God as he works his grace and peace down into the fabric of our lives.

Lesson one: Contentment can be learned. God is at work and he is the master teacher.

Lesson two: Coveting is off limits.

Lesson three: God will provide.

Your times of testing may not look anything like the stories I have shared. I trust that mine at least illustrate or bring to mind examples that may be closer to your experiences, where you live. Take some time to reflect upon some of your personal times of testing. Maybe you have observed someone who has gone through a unique period of testing that you can identify with and from whom you can learn.

Believing that God will provide what you need is a major lesson in the school of contentment. Keeping focused on this truth is one of the keys to learning contentment. When circumstances shout for your attention and try to distract, it is time to return to the simple truth that God is able to provide and he has promised to do so. Your job is to rest in him, believing that he is at work, and thrust yourself upon his mercy. The Bible says that we are to "consider it joy" because God delights in producing persevering faith in his followers during times of testing (James 1:1-3, 12).

Reflection Questions and Small Group Activities:

1.   What tests have you faced in the past?

2.   Can you see how God has been faithful to provide for you in the past?

3.   Are you currently facing any tests that call for a response of faith?

4.   Can you think of a time or situation when you experienced God's gift of peace?

5.   What is your greatest resistance point to trusting God's hand in your circumstances?

6.   Do a group activity listing the top ten most common tests that people in your age group face.

7.   Why do you think God placed Abraham and his test with Isaac so prominently in Scripture?

Prayer:

Lord, Grant us the wisdom to see what you are doing during times of testing. Teach us to see the events of our lives from heaven's perspective, to live by faith and rest in your wisdom and loving care. Give us the gift of your peace through your Son the Lord Jesus Christ in whose name we pray, amen.

Chapter 4

A Hungry Heart

"As the deer pants for streams of water, so my soul pants for you, O God. My soul thirsts for God, for the living God. When can I go and meet with God?" Psalm 42:1-2

Conventional wisdom says that contentment is being satisfied with your circumstances. This is not a bad definition but it does not go deep enough. It gives away too much and stops short of the real issue. It risks becoming fixated on circumstances and leads to the error of trying to manipulate God into giving you what you think will make you happy. "Delight yourself in the Lord and he will give you the desires of your heart" (Psalm 37:4) and similar promises become misunderstood and misused. The question becomes how much "delighting" do I have to do to get my circumstances changed – to get God to give me what I want (the real desire of my heart)? Most people think religion is finding the secret magic formula for getting God to provide them that which they believe will make them happy. This is based on the erroneous belief that happiness and contentment come from having ideal circumstances. True contentment, however, is an issue of the heart that goes beyond circumstances. It comes from a love relationship with God that transcends circumstances.

The Puritan Jeremiah Burroughs defined contentment in *The Rare Jewel of Christian Contentment*. "Christian contentment is that sweet, inward, quiet, gracious frame of spirit, which freely submits to and delights in God's wise and fatherly disposal in every condition."[2]

The question now becomes how can your heart be changed so that you can love God with all your heart as the "greatest commandment" (Matthew 22:36-38) demands, regardless of circumstances? How can you refocus yourself so that you truly delight in the Lord and are content with God and God alone? Solomon was right when he wrote, "Watch over your heart with all diligence, for from it flow the springs of life" (Proverbs 4:23 NASB). Solomon went on in the next few verses to give some great advice that he would have done well to heed himself.

A paraphrase of Proverbs 4:24 could read, don't lie. Stay away from twisting the truth. Lies do two things; 1) lies expose the true condition of the heart, and 2) lies influence the heart by reinforcing the wrong direction, thus hardening it. What can be done? First, you must acknowledge the truth, as revealed in the Bible, that only God can change your heart. You can cry out to him in repentance expressing belief in the truth of his promises (Romans 10:9-10, 17). Second, you can rehearse the truth as found in the Scriptures, reinforcing the dynamic of faith and looking to God to use his word and his Spirit to bring about the needed change. If you want your heart to change from bitter to sweet, you can respond

---

2
Jeremiah Burroughs, *Rare Jewel of Christian Contentment*, (Wilmington, Delaware: Sovereign Grace Pub.), 2.

to God's truth by putting it into practice and experience its transforming power.

You can lead your heart with your lips by speaking truth. The heart both leads the tongue and follows the tongue (Matthew 12:34). They influence each other. Let me illustrate.

1) Read or recite Scripture so that your heart can hear. I am amazed how reading the Bible out loud in private with no one else around affects me. It is very powerful. John Piper has written about the power of reading books aloud. "There is something about the living voice that quickens the truth and brings it home to us. You may find more power in your mouth than you dreamed, and your ears may open in ways that will change your life."[3]

2) Pray out loud in private as you confess your sin. Ask the Holy Spirit to bring to your attention the sin of coveting, and then confess it back to both God and your heart.

3) Give testimony to others of your desire to love and serve God. Let your heart listen to the conversation.

4) Practice reality checks. Speak your inner mental dialog out loud. Put your thoughts into words so that you can hear and clarify what is true and what is not. Ask yourself, is this thought entirely true? Am I exaggerating, overstating, twisting, or spinning the truth? This simple technique of putting thoughts into words by speaking them out loud often helps clarify and manage your thoughts. It also helps monitor the condition of the heart and helps transform both the mind and the heart. Invite the Holy Spirit to be an active participant in this process. Reality checks work best when God is invited into the process (Psalm 139:23).

3

John Piper, *A Godward Life*. (Sisters, OR: Multnomah Pub., 1997), 311.

In summary, leading your heart with your lips is quite simple, think and pray out loud so that you can hear and better understand your thoughts. Pour out your heart to God in prayer. A sample prayer could contain these words. O Lord, I desire to love you with all of my heart. Help my weak and vacillating faith. I confess my habit of discontentment, self-centeredness and hopelessness. I confess that only by your grace can I have a changed heart that follows you completely. Do the promised work of the New Covenant in me. Let the Spirit of God create a new heart within me. Continue to transform me into the likeness of Christ, reflecting ever more increasingly God's glory (Ezekiel 36:26-27, 2 Corinthians 3:18).

Solomon next moves from the lips to the eyes. "Let your eyes look straight ahead, fix your gaze directly before you" (Proverbs 4:25). The Bible often uses the metaphor of the eyes as a gate to the heart. Like the lips, the eyes can lead the heart. Guard your vision. Be careful what you focus upon. Solomon was right. You can direct your heart through giving careful attention to the direction and object of your gaze. The writer of the book of Hebrews understood this, "Let us fix our eyes on Jesus, the author and perfecter of our faith" (Hebrews 12:2). Jesus said it this way when he spoke about the importance of the eye. "The eye is the lamp of the body. If your eyes are good, your whole body will be full of light. But if your eyes are bad, your whole body will be full of darkness. If then the light within you is darkness, how great is that darkness! No one can serve two masters. Either he will hate the one and love the other, or he will be devoted to the one and despise the other. You cannot serve both God and Money" (Matthew 6:22-24). Just as the lips can lead the heart, so can the eyes.

You can fill your gaze with the things advertized in this world to bring contentment or you can determine to fill your mind's eye with Jesus and the things above. David stated the negative well when he said, "I will set no worthless thing before my eyes" (Psalm 101:3 NASB). David learned the hard way the importance of setting clear limits for his eyes. His sin with Bathsheba started with a look. The advertising world of marketing and the visual media is more than ready to set the agenda for your heart that will keep you in a constant state of discontentment. Advertisers know that the eyes of man are never satisfied (Proverbs 27:20). They work this principle again and again, sale after sale. The constant stream of new and improved, bigger and better products that promise to make life better and give more satisfaction and contentment is unending. Guard your vision; it is a gateway to the heart.

Job understood the importance of this principle when he said, "I made a covenant with my eyes not to look lustfully at a girl" (Job 31:1). The Bible uses the word lust to describe sexual greed. When lust is fed it becomes a powerful force that leads to the sins of fornication, sexual immorality and adultery. Jesus said that these spring from the heart (Matthew 15:19) fueled by a false belief that these activities will provide happiness and contentment. Yet in reality they bring just the opposite. They yield a harvest of pain and rob us of true contentment.

Paul stated very clearly, "It is God's will that you should be sanctified: that you should avoid sexual immorality; that each of you should learn to control his own body in a way that is holy and honorable, not in passionate lust like the heathen, who do not know God; and that in this matter no one should wrong his brother or take advantage of him. The Lord will punish men for all such sins, as we have already told you and warned you. For God did not call us to be impure, but to live a holy life" (1 Thessalonians 4:3-7). The word "sanctify" means to be holy or set apart for a special purpose. Contentment grows from an understanding and acceptance of God's purpose for you (Psalm 138:8). It is found in submitting to God's design for the creation and seeing your purpose within that plan. It matures when you limit yourself to stay within his revealed will and begin to enjoy the fruit of righteousness realizing that he has placed limits for where you seek wellbeing and happiness. It provides strength to resist the lie that God has held back something good from you. Satan continues to use the strategy of sowing doubts regarding the goodness of God as he did when he originally tempted Eve (Genesis 3:1-6). The seeds of discontentment often begin with doubts that God's intentions are good.

During this sabbatical time Bev and I have spent many hours listening to good preaching over the Internet. Alistair Begg[4] has been one of our favorites. These sermons have been a great encouragement and challenge to us. Reading books that exalt Jesus are also a great source for directing and refreshing the heart through the use of the eyes and ears. Without doubt the greatest and most effective way to focus your heart on God is by reading and studying his word. There is no substitute for cultivating the discipline of reading the Bible for keeping your eyes and your heart focused in the right direction. A few months ago I set a personal goal to read through the Bible in 40 days. I had never done that before in such a short time. Again the sabbatical provided the time and freedom to focus on this project. I was surprised how many new thoughts came as a result of that experience. I gained many new and fresh perspectives on old familiar stories. It was very profitable and

---

4

Alistair Begg, Truth for Life, http://www.truthforlife.org

I noticed a difference in my contentment level as I focused my attention on "things above" rather than worrying about "earthly things" (Philippians 3:19-20).

We have looked at the use of the lips and eyes to lead the heart. Now let's think about the metaphor of our feet. Solomon goes on to say, "Make level paths for your feet and take only ways that are firm. Do not swerve to the right or the left; keep your foot from evil" (Proverbs 4:26-27). Watch your step. Stay on the right path. Behavior affects your heart. There are behaviors that should be added and others that must be avoided if you want to guard your heart and learn contentment. Jesus' teaching is clear, "I tell you, do not worry" Matthew 6:25). "Seek first his kingdom and his righteousness" (v.33). "Do not store up for yourselves treasures on earth…but store up for yourselves treasures in heaven…for where your treasure is, there your heart will be also" (vv. 19-21). Jesus was speaking about behaviors that set the direction of the heart. You can invest in heaven and the desires of your heart will follow. Or you can invest in stuff here that rusts, wears out and gets stolen and your heart will experience worry and discontentment.

Bev and I have downsized three times and we still have too much stuff. Things can easily become an encumbrance that bog us down and keep us prisoners. Every time we move I am reminded how quickly the memorabilia, keepsakes, Christmas decorations, and tools fill up the boxes. The worst culprits are my precious books and I always forget how heavy they are. On one recent move we thought we could save some expense by renting a smaller truck. After working hard for half a day in the heat and humidity with the help of friends and family we were able to jam almost everything in to the back of the rental truck. It was packed to the roof. We congratulated ourselves on a job well done and it felt good. I decided it might be a good idea to weigh it before hitting the road just in case it was over the legal gross vehicle weight. I didn't want to have a problem at the truck scales along the way. We would be traveling through five states. You guessed it; it was two tons over weight. We called the rental company, got a bigger truck and spent the rest of the day transferring everything in the hot afternoon sun. Our short-lived satisfaction and contentment from doing a good job of packing the truck, quickly turned into frustration and embarrassment caused by my miscalculation.

We often miscalculate what will bring contentment. The belief that possessions will provide contentment is one of the most common mistakes that we make. Our consumer society reinforces this idea. But possessions eventually disappoint. At best they only provide short-term contentment. True long-term contentment is learned one step at a time, one eternal investment after another, not by the accumulation of earthly things that will pass away. There is a progressive learning curve that comes through experience and often includes some setbacks. We must be prepared to persevere even when the progress appears slow and halting.

Learning from others is wise. John Piper's books have been a great help and challenge to me. I would highly recommend them. Piper draws heavily upon the experiences and writings of Augustine, Luther, Calvin, Edwards and others in their pursuit of God and finding him alone satisfying.[5] Learn

---

5

John Piper, *The Legacy of Sovereign Joy*. (Wheaton, IL: Crossway Books, 2000), and *God's Passion for His Glory*. (Wheaton, IL: Crossway Books, 1998). Other John Piper books at, http://www.DesiringGod.org

to stand on the shoulders of those who have gone before and blazed a clear trail in the forest. The writings of the Reformers and the Puritans are gold mines that should not be overlooked. It is a mistake to consider them as outdated or avoided because of their sometimes laborious writing style.

The Bible, however, is the greatest compass, pointing the way to finding contentment in God alone. Meditating on the rich passages that the Holy Spirit has inspired is the place to begin. Stay camped in the green pastures beside the still water where your soul is well fed. Humbly ask the Spirit of God to instruct as you read the biblical record of those who wrote of their experiences with God.

Rather than longing to be somewhere else, note the words of David as he spoke of his contentment with God's sovereign placement, his acknowledgement of direction for the right path and anticipation of fullness of joy and eternal pleasures in God's eternal presence. "Lord, you have assigned me my portion and my cup, you have made my lot secure. The boundary lines have fallen for me in pleasant places; surely I have a delightful inheritance…You have made known to me the path of life; you will fill me with joy in your presence, with eternal pleasures at your right hand" (Psalm 16:5-6, 11).

In another Psalm, David gave testimony not only to God's blessings that satisfy on this earth but also to the anticipation of those blessings that await in heaven. "You still the hunger of those you cherish; their sons have plenty, and they store up wealth for their children. And I – in righteousness I will see your face; when I awake, I will be satisfied with seeing your likeness" (Psalm 17:14b-15). One of the greatest mistakes that we can make is to look for all of our contentment and reward in this lifetime and not long for heaven and what Christ has prepared for us.

During a difficult desert experience, David's prayer was a lucid statement of faith and experience of both soul thirst and satisfaction. "O God, you are my God, earnestly I seek you; my soul thirsts for you, in a dry and weary land where there is no water. I have seen you in the sanctuary and beheld your power and your glory. Because your love is better than life, my lips will glorify you. I will praise you as long as I live, and in your name I will lift up my hands. My soul will be satisfied as with the richest of foods; with singing lips my mouth will praise you" (Psalm 63:5).

Moses' prayer echoed the same longing when he said; "Satisfy us in the morning with your unfailing love, that we may sing for joy and be glad all our days" (Psalm 90:14).

The sons of Korah wrote a corporate (yet personal) expression of worship for the people of Israel during a very difficult time. "As the deer pants for streams of water so my soul pants for you, O God. My soul thirsts for God, for the living God. When can I go and meet with God" (Psalm 42:1-2)?

In another testimony from the hymnal of Israel used for collective worship we read instruction to find satisfaction in God's unfailing love. "Let them give thanks to the LORD for his unfailing love and his wonderful deeds for men, for he satisfies the thirsty and fills the hungry with good things" (Psalm 107:8-9).

In the New Testament we find the words of Jesus promising satisfaction and contentment for the thirsty soul. "Jesus answered, 'Everyone who drinks this water will be thirsty again, but whoever drinks the water I give him will never thirst. Indeed, the water I give him will become in him a spring of water welling up to eternal life'" (John 4:13-14). "Then Jesus declared, 'I am the bread of life. He who comes to me will never go hungry, and he who believes in me will never be thirsty'" (John 6:35). "If anyone is thirsty, let him come to me and drink. Whoever believes in me, as the Scripture has said, streams of living water will flow from within him" (John 7:37b-38). And the resurrected Christ speaking to John said, "To him who is thirsty I will give to drink without cost from the spring of the water of life" (Revelation 21:6b).

At the end of the Bible, the Holy Spirit and the Bride of Christ, the Church, repeat the invitation to all who have thirsty souls to come and drink. "The Spirit and the bride say, 'Come!' And let him who hears say, 'Come!' Whoever is thirsty, let him come; and whoever wishes, let him take the free gift of the water of life" (Revelation 22:17).

Lesson one: Contentment can be learned. God is at work and he is the master teacher.

Lesson two: Coveting is off limits.

Lesson three: God will provide.

Lesson four: Only God can truly satisfy. "Delight yourself in the Lord" (Psalm 37:4).

Reflection Questions and Small Group Activities:

1. What practical steps can you take to increase your hunger for God?

2. What secondary pursuits have gotten in the way of your focus on God alone as the source of ultimate contentment?

3. What evidence can be seen in your life that God is your greatest delight?

4. How can we assist others (each other) to be hungry for God?

5. List the top five things that people commonly try to use (mistakenly) as substitutes to fill their hunger for God.

6. How could Solomon write such good advice for directing the heart and yet fail so badly?

7. What Scripture passages or verses stood out in this chapter?

Prayer:

Lord, we acknowledge that we are not skilled in managing our inner life. Our eyes, our feet and our hearts too often run after the wrong things. We need your help. Increase our hunger and thirst for you, the source of all satisfaction. Draw us to yourself. Teach us to quiet our souls and be content in you. We pray in Jesus' name, amen.

Chapter 5

Risks Along the Way

*"When I fed them, they were satisfied; when they were satisfied,
they became proud; then they forgot me." Hosea 13:6*

There is a stretch of interstate 80 in the mountains out of
Laramie, Wyoming, that is posted with many huge warning
signs that patiently flash the need for caution during periods
of high wind and bad weather. The posted speed, when lights
are flashing is 45 miles per hour, which is painfully slow after
driving for hours at 70-75 mph. I was hoping to stay ahead
of a long line of trucks on a recent trip. It was one of those
times when the traffic in the right lane is too slow and the
left lane is too fast. The speed warnings were in effect and
it was starting to snow, one of those late spring storms that
was wet and slushy. It doesn't take much accumulation and
speed to cause your tires to suddenly hydroplane and lose
traction. A good strategy is to stay in the tire tracks cleared by
the big rigs. Pulling out into the left lane to pass, you can feel
the increased drag of resistance that can grab a tire and spin
you out of control if you have too much speed. In addition,
the wind was starting to howl off the mountain and the snow
was blowing across the road and beginning to build and
pack in places. Hitting one of these slick spots can take you
by surprise. I was tired from a long day on the road and I
was tempted to rationalize the conditions. "This isn't too bad
and I am an experienced driver in snow" - that is, until I
rounded a curve and saw an accident of an overturned
vehicle that had succumbed to the hazardous conditions.
I immediately slowed to a safer speed and pulled into the

slower right lane behind a truck. Why had I waited? I had underestimated the risk and dismissed the warnings until I saw the results of an accident.

Paul said that "things happened" to Israel in the Old Testament for a reason and that they were recorded to serve as "examples" and "warnings for us" (1 Corinthians 10:11). The Bible records many accidents that should grab our attention. We can learn from others' misfortunes and mistakes just as I had in the mountains of Wyoming.

An incident that stands out in the history of Israel is the account of the peoples' journey through the desert after leaving Mount Sinai. They began craving meat even though God had provided them with a special "heavenly food" called manna. God had wonderfully redeemed them out of slavery in Egypt, led them safely across the Red Sea and provided water in the wilderness. But the people "complained about the hardships" (Numbers 11:1) and craved food other than what God had supplied. They said, "if we only had meat to eat" (v. 4) and "we have lost our appetite; we never see anything but this manna" (v. 6).

This story is used a number of times later in the Bible to instruct and illustrate spiritual truth. Asaph's teaching is one such example. He said, "They ate till they had more than enough, for he had given them what they craved. But before they turned from the food they craved, even while it was still in their mouths, God's anger rose against them" (Psalm 78:29-31). And another description of the same event reads, "In the desert they gave in to their craving; in the wasteland they put God to the test. So he gave them what they asked for, but sent a wasting disease upon them" (Psalm 106:14-15). The last phrase can be translated, "but he sent leanness into their soul" (NKJV). Not everything I want and ask for is good for me.

Several important things stand out from this brief story. Note how quickly giving into their craving, turned into gluttony; "they ate till they had more than enough" (Psalm 78:29). When a person tries to fill his or her soul by indulging the stomach (or any other bodily appetite) it rapidly leads to excess and abuse. Abuse often follows when a person deviates from God's intended purpose. Abuse is about misuse. It is about trying to find satisfaction in something other than God. It is also about control. Abuse is about using power to control for the purpose of gaining personal satisfaction. It is an attempt to take that which is outside of God's revealed will and use it for selfish purposes. But it is also about losing the ability to control one's own behavior. Whenever you step outside of God's will you begin to lose your freedom. This is particularly true regarding food and sex.

Sin always carries consequences; there is a price to pay. One consequence is enslavement. "I tell you the truth, everyone who sins is a slave to sin" (John 8:34, Romans 6:16). This is true in several respects. First, man cannot free himself from the moral and spiritual penalty of sin. Only Christ's atoning sacrifice can set a person free from sin's penalty. Notice God's immediate reaction of displeasure. "God's anger rose against them" (Psalm 78:31). God's wrath rightfully falls upon any that come short of his standard of holiness and righteousness. The good news is that the penalty was paid by Jesus Christ on the cross and God's wrath was appeased when it was poured out upon the Lamb of God in his ministry of propitiation (1 John 2:2).

Second, man cannot free himself from the practice of sin apart from the intervention of God's grace and empowering ministry of the Holy Spirit. The effects of the slavery of sin run deep. It is true that the person who has been united with Christ (Romans 6:5-7) has been set free from sin's power.

The basis for this freedom is Christ's death and our spiritual participation with him in it. Paul goes on to say that we are to consider or reckon this to be true, "count yourselves dead to sin but alive to God in Christ Jesus" (v. 11). Freedom from the practice of sin comes as you offer or yield yourself to God (v. 12-14).

Our culture may make light of or even glorify giving in to various cravings (much of our society's entertainment celebrates the thrill of watching others succumb to evil cravings), but from God's perspective it is a most serious matter. It is an offence against his holy character and calls for his just wrath.

Greed is a very serious matter. The sin of unbridled indulging in greed by people who call themselves followers of God is an indication that they have turned their hearts away from him to substitutes, looking to other things in their pursuit of satisfaction. It calls into question their true relationship to God. Notice that "the greedy" are included in the list of those who "will not inherit the kingdom of God" (1 Corinthians 6:9-10).

Greed leads to a "wasting disease" of the soul. It is easy to allow your eyes to drift away from the God who supplies all good things and to simply crave the gifts that he provides. We may quote Paul's statement, "God, who richly provides us with everything for our enjoyment" but tend to forget the warning in the first half of the verse that says, "Command those who are rich in this present world not to be arrogant nor to put their hope in wealth, which is so uncertain, but to put their hope in God" (1 Timothy 6:17). Greed and covetousness can sneak up on the unsuspecting and thus calls for vigilance.

John Piper in his book Future Grace defines covetousness as "desiring something so much that you lose your contentment in God. Or: losing your contentment in God so that you start to seek it elsewhere."[6]

Money is not the only thing that can draw your heart away from God and spoil true contentment. It can be anything that distracts us from pursuing God with a whole heart. Even good things like hobbies, sports, career advancement, an academic degree, a business venture, shopping, or working out at the gym can distract us and become substitutes for God. Solomon's life story is instructive here. The book of Ecclesiastes is considered to be a testimony of his striving after many different things in an attempt to find meaning and satisfaction. His wealth and power gave him the opportunity to indulge his desires in an almost unlimited manner and he discovered that it was all empty or vanity. Note that Scripture concludes that it was the objects of his pursuits (the 700 foreign wives of royal birth, plus 300 concubines) that "turned his heart after other gods, and his heart was not fully devoted to the LORD his God...he did not follow the LORD completely" (1 Kings 11:4, 6).

Looking to anything or any person other than God for contentment is dangerous. For a woman it might be the idea that marriage to the perfect man will bring contentment. A man may desire the perfect women. I am reminded of a leader who was caught in an adulterous relationship and confided to me, "Lee, every time a woman walks through the door I look to see if she is the perfect woman that will satisfy all my needs." For years he entertained this common myth that

---

6

John Piper, *Future Grace*. (Sisters, OR: Multnomah Pub., 1995) 221.

many men indulge in their minds. His fantasy had set the trap and led him into adultery.

The myth that unlimited sexual exploits will bring satisfaction snared even Solomon with all his wisdom. This fantasy continues to seduce the unwary. Solomon's experience is a stark reminder that underscores the hazard of pursuing anything that detracts from the one thing that we were created for, intimacy with a holy God.

Success (for some) can be just as seductive as an extra marital affair. It can become an idol that robs of true riches by distracting from loving God with a whole heart. Benign desires for a promotion at work, a larger business, peer recognition or having the corner office can grow swiftly like a cancer and take over the heart. It doesn't matter if it's a secular career or the desires for success in ministry, both are susceptible to covetousness, greed and potential idolatry.

The pursuit of accomplishment placed ahead of intimacy with God can and will indeed lead to pride that elevates self, and attempts to dethrone God and squeeze him from his rightful place.

Lesson one: Contentment can be learned. God is at work and he is the master teacher.

Lesson two: Coveting is off limits.

Lesson three: God will provide.

Lesson four: Only God can truly satisfy.

Lesson five: Pursuing satisfaction in anything other than God is risky as it leads to pride, the sin of idolatry, loss of freedom, and deadness of soul that robs us of true contentment. "When I fed them, they were satisfied; when they were satisfied, they became proud; then they forgot me" (Hosea 13:6).

Reflection Questions and Small Group Activities:

1. What warning signs, cautions or risky behaviors have you been ignoring that have the potential to divert your heart from the pursuit of God?

2. What practical steps can you take to refocus your desire on God and God alone?

3. Who might you enlist as an accountability partner in these matters?

4. Have your small group list the top five risky behaviors that need warning signs.

5. Why do we continue to push the limits when we are aware of the dangers?

6. How can the members of your small group hold each other accountable to warning signs?

Prayer:

Father, help us to heed the warning signs that you have placed along the way. Forgive us for our pride that causes us to believe that we are exempt from the warnings and limits that you have placed for our own good. Help us to see the painful wreckage around us that we may be jolted by the reality of how high the stakes are for living within the moral boundaries that you have set for us in your Word. Empower us for righteous living that we may experience the contentment you have for us. In Jesus' name, amen.

Chapter 6

A Time to Run

*"But you, man of God, flee from all this, and
pursue righteousness, godliness, faith, love,
endurance and gentleness." 1 Timothy 6:11*

I run three or four days a week. It can hardly be called running
but on the coolness scale the term running has replaced
jogging. Running is in and jogging is out. Speed wise, what
I do is definitely slow jogging. The purpose of my running is
not to go anywhere, but to give my body a little workout and
to keep my body functioning at its full potential. I want to be
a good steward of what God has given me and that requires
consistency and work.

I wish I could say that I love to run. I don't. Unlike Eric
Liddell, the flying Scotsman of *Chariots of Fire*, I don't
particularly feel God's pleasure when I run. It is more like a
dreaded chore for me. My doctor says I need to push myself,
so I do it. As good as walking is, apparently it isn't enough
exertion for me. I also need the self discipline. My point is,
running needs a purpose that is worth the effort, or we won't
do it. We can run for health. We can run to get someplace in
a hurry, or we can run away from danger.

Metaphorically, the Bible says there is a time to run away.
It may sound cowardly but running away from temptation
has its place. It can be the very best strategy. The story of
Joseph escaping from the sexual advances of Potiphar's wife
comes to mind. "But he left his cloak in her hand and ran
out of the house" (Genesis 39:12). A good flight from evil

or danger can sometimes be the best protection. In the New Testament, Paul gave instruction to "flee immorality" (1 Corinthians 6:18), "flee from idolatry" (1 Corinthians 10:14) and "the evil desires of youth" (2 Timothy 2:22). He also told young Timothy to "flee" as he instructed him regarding one of the erroneous ideas of the false teachers. They were teaching that godliness was "a means to financial gain" (1 Timothy 6:5). There was some truth in what they were teaching but they were twisting that truth into something dangerous that needed correction. Paul's guidance was twofold; pursue the right things and flee the wrong things. "But you, man of God, flee from all this, and pursue righteousness, godliness, faith, love, endurance and gentleness" (verse 11).

Notice that this advice to Timothy was in the context of important teaching about contentment. "But godliness with contentment is great gain. For we brought nothing into the world, and we can take nothing out of it. But if we have food and clothing, we will be content with that. People who want to get rich fall into temptation and a trap and into many foolish and harmful desires that plunge men into ruin and destruction. For the love of money is a root of all kinds of evil. Some people, eager for money, have wandered from the faith and pierced themselves with many griefs" (1 Timothy 6:6-10).

Writing to the Corinthian congregation Paul said, "flee from idolatry" (1 Corinthians 10:14) and to both Ephesus and Colosse he equated greed with idolatry (Ephesians 5:5, Colossians 3:5). When is the time to run? The answer is, before any harmless desire turns into idolatrous greed. Run before this happens. The applications here will be quite personal. A good strategy begins with monitoring your heart. You must become aware of what has the potential for drawing you away from pursuing God with a whole heart. For some it may include adjusting certain financial goals, for others downsizing lifestyle, rethinking housing or transportation needs or setting aside a hobby. It may mean reevaluating how you view your cherished assets and establishing a plan for investing in heaven. This is a tricky topic because what may be potentially idolatrous for one person might not be for the next. The time to flee is before you are in trouble, before your heart has been stolen away and you find yourself in bondage.

The parable that Jesus told about the rich fool who had a good crop and decided to tear down his barns and build bigger ones was not about the size of his barns or his success as a farmer. It was about how he viewed wealth. Jesus' teaching was plain and to the point. He said, "Watch out! Be on your guard against all kinds of greed; a man's life does not consist in the abundance of his possessions" (Luke 12:15). The seeds of greed can grow in all kinds of soil and be attached to all kinds of things (possessions, money, etc.). You must watch for early sprouts and take action. Don't wait for greed to put down roots or until it produces a harvest. That will be too late. Anticipate the danger and run.

Idolatry, greed and contentment, are issues of the heart that have to do with what you believe will bring satisfaction. Don't set your heart on things that will not satisfy. They will cost more than they are worth. They are far too risky as they place claims and demands on your soul. Jesus said, "What good will it be for a man if he gains the whole world, yet forfeits his soul? Or what can a man give in exchange for his soul?" (Matthew 16:26).

I have been a life-long basketball fan. I miss playing but still enjoy watching a good game. During the NBA play-offs it becomes clear which teams have both a good offense and a good defense. A team can get by in the regular season with good offense alone and win a lot of games but during the playoffs they fade. The old saying is true, "defense wins championships." When it comes to greed, you need to have a good defense and a good offense. Paul's strategy for a good defense was to "flee." The second half of Paul's counsel and instruction to Timothy was to have a good offence, "pursue righteousness, godliness, faith, love, endurance and gentleness" (1 Timothy 6:11).

James wrote, "Come near to God and he will come near to you" (James 4:8). Coming near is about cultivating intimacy with Christ. Spending time in his presence in the relational activities of prayer and meditating on God's word is how this takes place. It is where you come to love the things that he loves. It is where you nurture a love for "righteousness, godliness, faith, love, endurance, and gentleness." because these are on his heart. These are defining characteristics (partial list) of who God is and they should define his sons and daughters as well. As you submit to his sovereign leadership, these attributes will begin to appear and grow within you as will your realization of the experience of contentment. It begins to emerge as you pursue Christ. As you draw near to him, he draws near to you and your experience of contentment grows. The gentle work of the Holy Spirit increasingly shows as he produces in you the sweet fruit of the Spirit (James 4:8, Galatians 5:22-23).

Lesson one: Contentment can be learned. God is at work and he is the master teacher.

Lesson two: Coveting is off limits.

Lesson three: God will provide.

Lesson four: Only God can truly satisfy.

Lesson five: Pursuing satisfaction in anything other than God is risky.

Lesson six: Learn to run.

Don't just walk, but run away from any thing that distracts you from pursuing and pleasing Jesus, and run toward Christ. Paul said it well, "No one serving as a soldier gets involved in civilian affairs – he wants to please his commanding officer" (2 Timothy 2:4). "So we make it our goal to please him…for we must all appear before the judgment seat of Christ, that each one may receive what is due him for the things done while in the body, whether good or bad" (2 Corinthians 5:9-10).

Reflection Questions and Small Group Activities:

1. What specific changes in your priorities do you believe you need to make?

2. Are you aware of any potential idolatry issues that you need to acknowledge and flee?

3. What behaviors in your life please Jesus and demonstrate your love for him?

4. Why do you think Paul chose the running metaphor to teach about having a defensive strategy?

5. Discuss the importance of a balanced Christian life with both defensive and offensive strategies.

6. Ask for testimonies from your small group members to share practical examples of how they run toward Christ.

Prayer:

Father, give us a distaste for sin and a hunger for you. Help us to see the dangers of sin and give us the courage to take quick action to flee. Help us to run toward you that we may find refuge and strength in times of need and temptation. May we find our true satisfaction in knowing you, our Creator and Sustainer, in Jesus' name we pray, amen.

Chapter 7

Giving and Contentment

"It is more blessed to give than to receive." Acts 20:35

Giving to the poor is an important teaching in Scripture. As early as the book of Esther the Jews were instructed to include "giving gifts to the poor" during times of celebration (Esther 9:22).

In the wisdom literature of Israel there are seven references to "giving gifts to the poor" (Psalm 112:9, Proverbs 14:21, 22:9, 28:8, 27, 31:20). Although expressed in slightly different wording, each unmistakably points to giving to the needy as godly and wise behavior.

Daniel's advice to King Nebuchadnezzar of Babylon to repent and acknowledge the Most High God as sovereign included a challenge to show kindness to those in need as a symbol of repentance (Daniel 4:27).

In the New Testament, sharing with the needy appears to be a normal practice of spiritual piety, although sometimes flawed by those taking advantage for personal profit and prestige (Matthew 26:9, Mark 14:5, Luke 19:8, John 13:29, Acts 2:45, 4:34).

The gospel writers record two instances in four texts when Jesus said, "sell your possessions and give to the poor" (Matthew 19:16-29, Mark 10:17-30, Luke 12:33, 18:18-30). Three of these repeat the story of the rich young ruler. The point of the story is not about selling what you have and giving it away to earn salvation. Rather, Jesus appears to be exposing the young man's heart, showing him that he was a slave of his wealth and this bondage prevented him from following Jesus.

The fourth passage where Jesus said, "sell your possessions and give to the poor" (Luke 12:33) is not addressed to an individual but is a general command. Jesus is instructing his followers to live now, in the realization that, "your Father has been pleased to give you the kingdom" (v. 32). His purpose was to direct his disciples to focus on the kingdom of God. Jesus was teaching that giving is a means of directing one's heart toward heaven. A heart filled with preoccupation and worry is looking for contentment in things now on this earth. The main point is found at the end of the paragraph, "For where your treasure is, there your heart will be also" (v. 34). Giving steers the heart in the direction of heaven.

Lesson one: Contentment can be learned. God is at work and he is the master teacher.

Lesson two: Coveting is off limits.

Lesson three: God will provide.

Lesson four: Only God can truly satisfy.

Lesson five: Pursuing satisfaction in anything other than God is risky.

Lesson six: Learn to run.

Lesson seven: Be generous and give to those in need because it leads the heart to be kingdom minded.

It is true. "It is more blessed to give than to receive" (Acts 20:35). This was underscored by Jesus in his teaching about the shrewd manager when he said, "I tell you, use worldly wealth to gain friends for yourselves, so that when it is gone, you will be welcomed into eternal dwellings" (Luke 16:9). Jesus was not saying this is how one can earn an entrance ticket into heaven but rather that when you arrive in heaven there will be friends that you have helped who will warmly greet you and welcome you into your eternal home.

I have wrestled with how to implement this concept. To what projects and causes should I contribute? There are so many needs and requests that pull at my heart. Sometimes there are good reasons not to give or to give a token amount. My struggle often revolves around my perceptions of my limited resources and thinking that the amount of my gift would be too small to make any real difference. But Paul makes it clear that the important thing is not the amount but the willingness. He says, "For if the willingness is there, the gift is acceptable according to what one has, not according to what he does not have" (2 Corinthians 8:12). And Jesus' remarks are clear about the widow who gave two small copper coins, "this poor widow has put in more than all the others" (Luke 21:3).

A church leader cannot afford to rationalize that his role is solely to motivate others to give. This is especially tempting under the pressure of leading large building projects, capital funding improvements or when failing to meet budgets. Institutions will forever have financial needs. The risk is always present to emotionally manipulate people to give. One representative from a professional fund raising company told me, "You cannot build new buildings without large contributions and your job is to meet with and motivate those donors." But this kind of thinking loses sight of the purpose that giving is a means of directing the heart not necessarily solving budgetary problems or funding building projects.

I have observed that there are generally two groups of people, the givers and the takers. The old 80/20 rule seems to be quite true, that 80% of the work (and giving) is done by 20% of the people. After working in various ministry contexts for over 40 years serving as pastor of three churches and with three different mission agencies, I have found this to be sadly true in both church and missions. I have met many wonderful givers along the way. They tend, however, to be a minority. There always seem to be many more takers than givers.

The American church appears to have undergone a noticeable change in the last 50 years in its attitude toward money. As the Western world has become relatively wealthy, expectations regarding compensation and standard of living have changed. There is a growing sense of entitlement among all of us, including those in ministry. I have heard the argument expressed that to survive in ministry, one must learn to work the system to one's advantage. One mission leader cynically expressed to me, "It's all about the money" as he spoke about prevailing attitudes within his agency. It is becoming more common to find some who labor in the vineyard, living very well from the gifts of donors, while others are struggling to make ends meet. Resistance is encountered when attempting to establish greater fiscal accountability to meet the growing demands from accountants and auditors. When the topic is broached, the response is likely to be, "We've never had to do that before," or, a defensive reference to the verse, "'Do not muzzle the ox while it is treading out the grain,' and 'The worker deserves his wages'" (1 Timothy 5:18). I've even heard the attitude expressed, "If I raised it, I should be able to spend it." These are not-so-subtle symptoms of greed. To be sure, there are many examples of those in ministry with gracious spirits, who live frugally on meager allowances. A sea-change, however, has no doubt occurred from previous generations. A lowering tide makes all boats vulnerable to the rocks that are being exposed. Serious questions have emerged for the church in affluent America.

I fear that we stand at risk of being left without a clear and believable voice when speaking about the subject of materialism. Has affluence affected our moral authority to speak out about the spirit of greed that has crept into the church? Have we allowed ourselves to be squeezed into the financial patterns of the materialistic world around us? Paul said, "Do not conform any longer to the pattern of this world, but be transformed by the renewing of your mind. Then you will be able to test and approve what God's will is – his good, pleasing and perfect will" (Romans 12:2).

Jesus' words to the religious leaders of his day were particularly harsh and direct. He cautioned his disciples repeatedly and pointedly regarding the spiritual heart conditions of those in religious leadership. A study of what one could call the, "Watch out/Beware/Be on your guard" passages of Jesus are sobering (Matthew 6:1, 7:15, 10:17, 16:6, 26:41, Mark 13:5, 9, Luke 12:15, 17:3, 21:34, 21:36). These can be grouped into six general categories of warnings: 1) pride, 2) false teachers and the "yeast" of their false teachings, 3) dangers from men who can harm you, 4) temptation, spiritual alertness and issuing a call to watch and pray, 5) things that cause others to stumble and hearts weighted down with dissipation, and 6) greed. These can be further summarized into two major warnings that center on the subjects of the false teaching and the greed of the religious leaders.

One cannot help but be aware of the growing trend by many to teach a "prosperity gospel" that promises the pathway to wealth is through "giving" or just "claiming" it. As I travel among the churches in developing countries I find this message has reached the ends of the earth and is particularly harmful among young churches and new believers. This false theology was developed in America during a time of unrestrained greed within our culture and the church has simply been silent or joined in by repackaging greed with spiritually sounding smooth talk. Paul's warnings are particularly relevant today (1 Timothy 6:3-10, 2 Timothy 4:3-4).

About four years ago God began to do a new work in my life in the area of giving. During our married life we have always practiced giving a tithe, but God began to stretch our thinking. It started with a request from a church leader in India. At the time I was serving in leadership directing a small mission agency. The request was simple. Would our organization consider a funding request to support evangelists and church planters in India? The plan was to partner with an association of evangelicals representing all of India that reaches across denominational lines. They would select, train, send out and supervise workers in the villages where many were coming to Christ, often amid very real persecution. The individual workers could live on $50 per month. I thought this was a great idea, but I doubted that our board of directors would approve as it was outside the organizational charter. They voted to decline this request, but God would not let me rest. It was as if a new fire had been kindled, and it has since become one of the greatest delights of my life.

We started a foundation (Seed for the Sowers), that, by God's grace, supports 75 full-time workers in India. The reports we get back are some of the most thrilling I have ever experienced in ministry. In one recent ten-month period they reported 3,396 new believers, 2,937 baptisms, 154 new church plants or new gathering points, and 237 new workers trained. Bev and I have committed ourselves to give beyond what we ever thought would be possible and it has brought us a deep and satisfying joy, a real sense of contentment.

Leading up to the decision to start Seed for the Sowers,[7] God drew me to a number of passages of Scripture. I remember one particular sleepless night in a hotel in Bangkok, Thailand as I wrestled with Paul's instruction to the believers in Corinth. How should I personally apply his teaching where he said, "Our desire is not that others might be relieved while you are hard pressed, but that there might be equality" (2 Corinthians 8:13). Equality? We have so much more than these brothers who live on $50 per month, how can I ignore this request and not get involved?

Paul continued, "Then there will be equality, as it is written; 'He who gathered much did not have too much, and he who gathered little did not have too little'" (vv. 14-15). Paul is not promoting a state sponsored and controlled communism or socialism where property rights of individuals are violated. History has shown that when governments attempt to force economic equality is it ineffective. Greed is still present and those with less political power are exploited. Greed is capitalism's great flaw as well and we have witnessed plenty of shameful examples of exploitation in the last few years. The television show American Greed features one scam after another documenting the moral, legal and financial underbelly of Western capitalism.

7

Information regarding Seed for the Sowers can be found at www.seedforthesowers.com

Except for a few communal orders and collective societies, the church today generally ignores Paul's vision for equality. How should this teaching motivate and guide the American church to practice what Paul calls "grace" giving? What is our moral and spiritual responsibility to help believers from other geographic areas of the world who are struggling?

God kept bringing chapters eight and nine of 2 Corinthians back to my mind as he changed my heart and planted the seeds of this new vision. A key verse that stood out was, "Now he who supplies seed to the sower and bread for food will also supply and increase your store of seed and will enlarge the harvest of your righteousness" (2 Corinthians 9:10). Notice that there are three things one can do with seed: 1) you can grind it into flour, bake bread and eat it; 2) you can store it, or 3) you can plant it back into the ground. These are the three uses for money; consuming, savings, and investing. Paul is teaching that investing can be either for a harvest now or for an eternal harvest of righteousness. The verse also says that God will supply all three uses. I needed to see that God would supply for us to eat, to save (store for the future) and to give. Each category demands living by faith and requires that God's wisdom guide us to be good stewards of what he supplies. We need to remember that he owns it all. We continue to learn as a couple.

During the years leading up to my 65th birthday I found myself worrying about saving enough for retirement. The more I worried the less content I became. That was wrong, because God has promised to supply our needs. It is interesting that Paul's testimony, "I can do everything through him who gives me strength" (Philippians 4:13) is in the context of Paul's statement about being content. And his equally famous declaration, "And my God will meet all your needs according to his glorious riches in Christ Jesus" (v.19) was written in the context of giving. Contentment and giving are inseparably linked in God's economy. I needed to learn more about contentment in the arena of economic transition. Faith is stretched while learning to live with less income yet trusting God for wisdom to practice generosity in giving.

Much of the focus on saving in America is for retirement. Some have said that retirement is not in the Bible and should not be part of our thinking. The Lord, however, gave Moses instruction for the Levites' retirement. "This applies to the Levites: Men twenty-five years old or more shall come to take part in the work at the Tent of Meeting, but at the age of fifty, they must retire from their regular service and work no longer. They may assist their brothers in performing their duties at the Tent of Meeting, but they themselves must not do the work" (Numbers 8:23-26). Some might dismiss this as no longer relevant because it is taken from the Old Testament Law, but are there principles and wisdom that we can draw from it for application today? What can we learn from this Scripture?

God provided a set age for a legitimate stepping aside from the burden of the work while allowing those who desired to remain active to have a helping role. Note that a role change was required. Today there are many issues that can necessitate a role change including age, declining health, diminished capacity, or changing demands in the work place. One should also honestly examine to what degree his or her identity and social standing muddles the judgment. Titles, positions and pay scale can influence motivation. Finances, ego, guilt, fear, power or pride are real issues we all face.

The church needs to provide a biblically clear voice to address this subject beyond the normal binary thinking of either on or off, all or nothing, retired or full-time. We need to develop a more helpful biblical view of retirement and the contribution of older adults.

A few years ago we sat in an older adult Sunday school class. Following an impassioned plea for help in the children's ministry we heard people voicing a common sentiment, "We've paid our dues. Been there. Done that. Let the younger people do it." We must guard against the kind of self-centered attitude displayed by the rich fool of Jesus' parable who said, "And I'll say to myself, 'You have plenty of good things laid up for many years. Take life easy; eat, drink and be merry'" (Luke 12:19).

Another important passage in the Bible that should be considered on this topic is Jesus' statement, "Be dressed ready for service and keep your lamps burning like men waiting for their master to return" (Luke 12:35). This does not necessarily mean working in a salaried position until Christ returns or that we must die in the saddle, but it does clearly teach a continued readiness for service. There are many creative ways to stay age-appropriately engaged and making a contribution for the kingdom. Prayer and giving are two obvious ministries that have no age restrictions. Mentoring younger leaders, sharing the wisdom gained through life, making repairs, pulling weeds, taking meals to shut-ins, visiting those in care facilities, providing a grandparent role for a single parent or within a children's Sunday school class are but a few. Some times the greatest blessing an older adult can provide is to provide a genuine listening ear, taking the time to show interest and to pray specifically for a younger person. New models should be developed to explore and take advantage of the experience and expertise of senior citizens.

Another relevant passage is the parable of the talents (Luke 19:11-27). Jesus is teaching that we should take advantage of opportunities and display an entrepreneurial spirit by investing wisely with an expectation of a good return. The parable also reinforces the truth that all resources and opportunities that we have in life are provided by God. They are ultimately his. We are merely stewards of these for a time. They have been entrusted to us for the purpose of using them for eternal gain. He will ask us to give an account for what we have done with them.

The faith-centered life of a Christian senior citizen should not be filled with worrying about having enough bread to eat or bragging about having a barn full of savings. We should have a faith plan for investing treasure in heaven at every age in life. Jesus' words ought to guide us as we learn the lesson that giving directs the heart and aids in finding true contentment (Luke 12:13-34).

Reflection Questions and Small Group Activities:

1. What do you worry about that steals your contentment?

2. Review how you are managing your three uses of money: consuming, saving and investing.

3. What steps can you take to develop a giving plan to invest treasure in heaven?

4. How can you implement Paul's "equality" concept into your life?

5. How can we help each other think more biblically about all of life's stages?

6. Ask for testimonies from your group about giving lessons that individuals have learned.

7. How can we answer the question, "How much is enough?"

Prayer:

Lord, give us a healthy godly view of work and giving. Help us to learn to direct our hearts toward heaven by giving to those who have need. Teach us to follow your leadership in wisely managing the amounts of seed we consume, save and invest for eternity. Thank you for providing sufficiently for each. Help us to find more contentment in giving than earning or consuming. Give us the perspective of heaven, we pray in Jesus' name, amen.

Chapter 8

Comparisons

*"I want to test the sincerity of your love by comparing
it with the earnestness of others." 2 Corinthians 8:8*

*"When they measure themselves by themselves
and compare themselves with themselves, they
are not wise." 2 Corinthians 10:12*

The two verses quoted at the beginning of this chapter, at
first glance, could appear to be incompatible. Paul made
comparisons with the Macedonian churches to motivate
the Corinthians to give and then later said it was unwise
for the false teachers to make comparisons. Was he being
inconsistent? Both of Paul's statements are in 2 Corinthians
and are found only two chapters apart. We must sort this
out if we are to explore how making comparisons affects the
topic of contentment.

First, making comparisons is risky. It often leads to judging
others and a spirit of judging often leads to discontentment.
Jesus, Paul and James all warned against judging (Matthew
7:1, Romans 14:1, 10, James 4:12). Paul rightfully warns
about the dangers of making comparisons as the false teachers
were doing. "When they measure themselves by themselves
and compare themselves with themselves, they are not wise"
(2 Corinthians 10:12). It is not wise. I will explore in
more detail later in this chapter the link between making
comparisons and contentment.

Second, Paul was writing under the inspiration of the Holy Spirit when he used comparison language to teach and motivate the church in Corinth to give. "I want to test the sincerity of your love by comparing it with the earnestness of others" (2 Corinthians 8:8). He waxed eloquent about the Macedonians' "rich generosity" in giving to the needs of the believers in Jerusalem (vv. 1-5). We can safely conclude that there is a place for learning from the example of others. The Bible includes much instruction for us that is illustrated by good and bad examples. Comparisons and contrasts between righteousness and unrighteousness help clarify between good and evil. Learning from comparisons can be informative and helpful but still it can be risky.

Third, we need to remember Jesus' reminder about the risks of making comparisons when he taught about giving in secrecy. "So when you give to the needy, do not announce it with trumpets, as the hypocrites do in the synagogues and on the streets, to be honored by men. I tell you the truth, they have received their reward in full. But when you give to the needy, do not let your left hand know what your right hand is doing, so that your giving may be in secret. Then your Father, who sees what is done in secret, will reward you" (Matthew 6:2-4).

Jesus was teaching about wrong motivation for giving. "Be careful not to do your acts of righteousness before men, to be seen by them" (v. 1). The key phrases here are "to be seen by them" and "to be honored by men" as this is what the hypocrites of Jesus' day were doing. This is the first of three examples that Jesus gave where people try to look righteous on the outside while not dealing with the heart. He warned about the misuse of giving, prayer and fasting. Hypocrites have tried to exploit all three of these good things over the centuries to give the appearance of righteousness. These activities can never earn an individual right standing before God. Jesus underscored this point in the preceding six points of his sermon (Matthew 5:21-48). He made it abundantly clear that the experts of the religious system had been using these religious activities to look good to others and appear to be something that they were not, but they were misjudging God's standard of righteousness. They had selfish motives.

We must be very careful to avoid doing good things with wrong motives. God sees the heart and one of the ways he exposes wrong motives is by removing contentment and replacing it with frustration and discontentment (Haggai 1:5-11).

You can see a person's outward behavior, but it is very difficult to see heart motivation. God sees both clearly. You can learn from another's behavior because you can see it. Unless God reveals heart motivation, you can only guess and speculate, and that is very dangerous. You can learn from hypocrites but only when God exposes their motivation. You do not see the heart as God sees it, therefore you must refrain from judging that which is hidden from your human eyes (Matthew 7:1). Jesus also said, "By their fruit you will recognize them" (v. 16). You can observe and learn from the futility, pain and frustration that result.

We can study and gain insight about the dangers of hypocrisy because Jesus uncovered the heart motivation of the religious leaders of his day. He opened their hearts and laid bare the issues of their hypocrisy. He exposed what they were doing for the sake of appearance. Hypocrisy is motivated by pride and ego elevation. Sometimes it shows itself by making comparison with others for the sake of appearing superior. This is what Paul was warning about when he said, "We do not dare to classify or compare ourselves with some who commend themselves. When they measure themselves by themselves and compare themselves with themselves, they are not wise" (2 Corinthians 10:12). The false teachers were making comparisons among themselves and with Paul. This is not only unwise, it is spiritually dangerous.

Now let's return to the link between making comparisons and its affects upon contentment and discontentment. We live in a day when making comparisons between preachers, musicians, size and philosophy of ministry, and almost everything else in the church, is as popular as the latest reality TV show. The habit of making comparisons is not limited to church. It is how business is done, the way schools function, the life-blood of sports, and the dynamic of popular entertainment programs like Survivor and American Idol. We live in a world that makes comparisons about everything.

I believe that there is a clear relationship between making comparisons and having a diminished capacity for experiencing contentment. The more you engage in making comparisons, the more discontentment you will experience. You will also find a growing temptation to shift your eyes from the outward behavior of others to judging their inward motivation. This crosses a line that is off limits. True contentment cannot coexist with a spirit of judging the motives of others. Remember – only God sees the heart and is qualified to make those judgments.

Here you must be "wise as serpents and harmless as doves" (Matthew 10:16 NKJV). You must understand how the motivational functioning of "bitter envy and selfish ambition" work (James 3:14-16), but refrain from engaging in their activities or attitudes (and from accusing others of participating). This is no easy task. I believe one key is to cultivate your confidence in the Holy Spirit's power to expose the heart and bring about conviction of sin, true righteousness and a realization of the coming judgement of all, (John 16:8) and leave the judging to him.

The more negative and aggressive you become in judging other's behavior and heart motivation the more you forfeit the sweet experience of contentment. Pride and humility also correlate with the tendency to judge. When pride increases there is an accompanying push toward discontentment and judging others. "God opposes the proud but gives grace to the humble" (1 Peter 5:5). Humility on the other hand softens and moves a person toward compassion and contentment and away from a spirit of judging. We are to cultivate humility and eradicate pride. Humility provides good soil in which contentment can grow. Pride displeases God and blunts the development and maturing of contentment.

When we engage in making seemingly harmless comparisons, (even at the behavioral level while avoiding judging motives), there is an increased risk for experiencing discontentment because it diverts your eyes from Jesus to yourself and others. It often leads to making evaluations that lead to disappointment or pride.

Lesson one: Contentment can be learned. God is at work and he is the master teacher.

Lesson two: Coveting is off limits.

Lesson three: God will provide.

Lesson four: Only God can truly satisfy.

Lesson five: Pursuing satisfaction in anything other than God is risky.

Lesson six: Learn to run.

Lesson seven: Give to those in need.

Lesson eight: Stop making comparisons. It erodes contentment and leads to all kinds of wrong judgment and discontentment.

Reflection Questions and Small Group Activities:

1. In what areas of your life are you most prone to making harmful comparisons?

2. How can you learn from others' behaviors without becoming jealous, critical or proud?

3. Can you think of any situations when your discontentment grew as a result of making comparisons?

4. List and discuss examples of how our society makes comparisons.

5. Ask for testimonies from your small group regarding positive lessons learned from watching the behavior of others.

6. Explore the risks of trying to judge the heart motives of others. Why are we so prone to do it?

Prayer:

Father, forgive us for making comparisons among ourselves and judging one another. Teach us to stimulate one another to love and good works. Deliver us from the pride and jealousy that enslaves, and grant us the freedom to rest in our right standing in Jesus Christ in whose name we pray, amen.

Chapter 9

Wasting Away and Being Renewed

"Therefore we do not lose heart. Though outwardly we are wasting away, yet inwardly we are being renewed day by day." 2 Corinthians 4:16

Pain is an unwelcome reality of life. I do not like to face physical discomfort. I don't like back pain, headaches, hangnails or going to the dentist. In fact I do not like discomfort of any kind.

I had known for some time that my heart disease was getting worse, but I didn't want to face the possibility of open heart surgery. The idea of ripping my chest open and all that's involved didn't appeal to me in the least. For several years I had been self-monitoring the three major symptoms of heart disease: shortness of breath, fatigue and chest pain. I found that I could push myself to the point of angina (chest pain) by running too fast. I discovered this while staying at a hotel in India. I was using a treadmill provided in the exercise room, trying to stay in shape; something that is always difficult to do while traveling. The controls of the treadmill were in kilometers per hour rather than miles and I inadvertently miscalculated my speed and set my pace too fast. I began to have some chest discomfort that lasted most of the day. Later I figured it out and began to experiment to find out at what speed the pain would start. This was not very smart, but being a curious person I thought I would find my ceiling and stay under that speed. It was like doing my own stress test. I was already working hard at eating right and monitoring emotional stress but I also knew that I was losing ground in my battle with heart disease.

Thirteen years earlier I had my first heart episode and the intervention of balloon angioplasty had worked. Now my doctor (who had become a good friend) insisted that I see the cardiologist again for evaluation. Once I gave in, things moved quickly and I didn't have much time to worry about the pain involved. The angiogram showed that a stent would not do the job and my resistance to doing the CABG (cardio artery by-pass graft) procedure weakened in light of hard visual evidence on the monitor and strong medical advice.

The surgery and recovery went well. I thank God for the medical advances that can both fix many things and effectively manage pain. Looking back over the experience, I now realize that more than avoidance of pain was taking place. I think I was having difficulty accepting the "wasting away" process, as Paul put it. Aging is usually a slow process of losses with little crises along the way. We lose a little here and a little there; the body is running down and wearing out. I have been very active throughout my life and accepting the reality of "wasting away" was not on my radar. Being content while we age is a challenge. The reality of heart disease was forcing me to face the contentment issue in yet another circumstance. Three months following the surgery, I was ready to send out my resume and get started looking for another ministry position. Bev wasn't so sure that this was a good idea, so we asked our family for some honest feedback and advice when we were together. What I heard from them sounded a little like a firm but loving intervention. They all agreed that it was too soon and I needed to wait, rest and finish healing. They were right. I was being impatient. It is not easy to stay in the sweet spot of contentment. It was also a good reminder of how much self-worth and contentment get linked to accomplishments, especially for action people like me.

There is something about the "wasting away" process of our bodies that pressures and tests faith, perseverance and contentment. As a pastor I have walked with many people through the experiences of illness, surgery, brokenness, loss and grief. I have watched God at work bringing about inner spiritual growth and maturity of faith in the midst of very hard times. I have also watched others who have despaired and walked away in anger and disillusionment, questioning God's goodness. I have often been reminded of Jesus' words explaining the meaning of the parable he told of the farmer sowing seed in different types of soil. "Those on the rock are the ones who receive the word with joy when they hear it, but they have no root. They believe for a while, but in the time of testing they fall away. The seed that fell among thorns stands for those who hear, but as they go on their way they are choked by life's worries, riches and pleasures, and they do not mature" (Luke 8:13-14). Notice the association Jesus makes between discontentment and those that lack maturity and perseverance. Can we draw the conclusion that contentment is a mark of true faith? If so, it is not optional or reserved for the super spiritual.

When Paul told the story of his hardships and trials to the Corinthians, he was able to say, "Therefore we do not lose heart. Though outwardly we are wasting away, yet inwardly we are being renewed day by day" (2 Corinthians 4:16). Surrounding this little verse I believe that we discover his secret for contentment. Paul had learned to manage his perspective. He understood that he was both reflecting God's glory and was "being transformed into his [Christ's] likeness with ever-increasing glory" (2 Corinthians 3:18). This knowledge gave him perspective to see his life experiences from an eternal vantage point. This is why he could say, "Therefore we do not lose heart." His heart and eyes were fixed on Jesus. He went on to say, "For our light and momentary troubles are achieving for us an eternal glory that far outweighs them all. So we fix our eyes not on what is seen, but on what is unseen. For what is seen is temporary, but what is unseen is eternal" (vv. 17-18). Keeping an eternal perspective is truly one of the most important secrets of learning contentment.

Pain can distract us, calling us to focus on the physical demands of the here and now experience, and tempting us to doubt and despair, or it can remind us that this body is wasting away; that our eternal home is but a breath away. In preparation for those times of pain and testing that will most certainly come to each of us, we need to fix our eyes on Jesus and the unseen spiritual reality of heaven and allow him to renew us day by day. Apart from God's work of transformation and the renewal of the inner person by the Holy Spirit, we would be left to decline as the years take their toll, acting like grumpy old men trying to hang on to fading memories of past glory. As Christians, however, we look forward, by faith, to all that God has in store for us as he works to put his finishing touches on our inner person, readying us for the glory that is about to be revealed at his soon coming.

Lesson one: Contentment can be learned. God is at work and he is the master teacher.

Lesson two: Coveting is off limits.

Lesson three: God will provide.

Lesson four: Only God can truly satisfy.

Lesson five: Pursuing satisfaction in anything other than God is risky.

Lesson six: Learn to run.

Lesson seven: Give to those in need.

Lesson eight: Stop making comparisons.

Lesson nine: Realize that outwardly you are wasting away, but inwardly you are being renewed.

Reflection Questions and Small Group Activities:

1. What physical maladies that are part of your current experience remind you that you are outwardly wasting away?

2. Have you experienced difficult times that have drawn you closer to Christ?

3. Are you experiencing any circumstances that are turning your eyes to the unseen realities of heaven?

4. What insights have you gained by meditating on 2 Corinthians 3:18 and 4:16?

5.   Why do we tend to be so preoccupied with our physical well-being, but so casual with our spiritual renewal? What does pain have to do with it?

6.   Why do you think some professing Christians become grumpy in later years while others become gentle, pleasant and godly?

7.   Draw up a sample mission statement or manifesto taking ideas from 2 Corinthians 4:16-18.

Prayer:

Father, as the flower fades and we lose the luster of youth, may we be reminded of the glory that is about to be revealed in us at Jesus' return. Forgive us for being so preoccupied with our aches and pains and so unconcerned with the inner renewal that you are accomplishing in us to prepare us for eternity. Grant us grace to face the wasting away process and faith to persevere until we receive our glorified bodies in the resurrection. In Jesus' name we pray, amen.

Chapter 10

Learning from Others

"I have stilled and quieted my soul; like a weaned child with its mother, like a weaned child is my soul within me." Psalm 131:2

People are interesting. Good novels are captivating because they are about people. While telling stories about people, they are descriptive and filled with fascinating character development. We meet some curiously odd people along the path of life. We like to read about them, look at them and talk about them. What would movies, plays and works of fiction be if writing about people was off limits? God has chosen to fill the Bible with stories of real people for the purpose of letting us look, listen and learn. We often learn as much from their mistakes as their successes.

Lesson one: Contentment can be learned. God is at work and he is the master teacher.

Lesson two: Coveting is off limits.

Lesson three: God will provide.

Lesson four: Only God can truly satisfy.

Lesson five: Pursuing satisfaction in anything other than God is risky.

Lesson six: Learn to run.

Lesson seven: Give to those in need.

Lesson eight: Stop making comparisons.

Lesson nine: Realize that outwardly you are wasting away but inwardly you are being renewed.

Lesson ten: Learn from the example of others.

In this chapter we will explore a variety of curiously odd examples from the Old Testament. I have chosen to include these particular characters because they each wrestled in some way with the issue of contentment.

Baruch served as Jeremiah's secretary. He wrote down the words of the prophecy on a scroll as Jeremiah dictated them. This means that he heard the messages of God's coming judgement before anyone else. It was a little like having insider trading information about the stock market, and it was about to crash. He wrote down the message that Jerusalem was soon to be destroyed and he reacted with a few choice words. He may have assumed that no one heard. That is, until God confronted him with what he had said, "This is what the LORD, the God of Israel, says to you, Baruch: You said, 'Woe to me! The LORD has added sorrow to my pain, I am worn out with groaning and find no rest'" (Jeremiah 45:2-3).

Baruch's name is taken from the Hebrew word "barak" and means "blessed by the Lord." His words indicate that he was not feeling very blessed. They show that he was grieving and experiencing painful sorrow. He was not enjoying a quiet rest and peace in his soul. Upon first glance one might say his response was logical and appropriately in line with the coming circumstances. But God exposed his heart and delivered a very personal message, "Should you then seek great things for yourself? Seek them not" (Jeremiah 45:5). Apparently Baruch had plans for himself. We know that he was from a prominent family and he must have had expectations for God to bless him just as his name suggested. His plans would be interrupted, if not completely scuttled. God did bless him by promising to spare his life, "but wherever you go I will let you escape with your life" (v. 5).

The way we respond when God reveals his sovereign will is a key challenge to living a life of contentment. This is especially true when our dreams are dashed. Baruch was probably a man of faith, but we are left with only six verses, recorded in one of the shortest chapters in the Bible, that chronicle his lapse into discontentment. Baruch is one of those curiously odd examples from whom we can learn. Baruch's life went from blessing to pain.

Jabez on the other hand went from pain to blessing. His name means pain, "His mother named him Jabez, saying, 'I gave birth to him in pain'" (1 Chronicles 4:9). What an awkward name to carry around! There are only two verses in the Bible about Jabez and one might wonder why they are included. Why is his story told? Jabez stood apart. He "was more honorable than his brothers" (v. 9). Rather than wallow in self-pity due to his painful circumstances, he expressed faith, "Jabez cried out to the God of Israel, 'Oh, that you would bless me and enlarge my territory! Let your hand be with me, and keep me from harm so that I will be free from pain.' And God granted his request" (v. 10). The Hebrew word used for "bless" is the word "barak" and thus you can see why the stories of Jabez and Baruch fit together and contrast each other. Jabez's life went from pain to blessing while Baruch's life went from blessing to pain.

There are several things we can learn from these two short stories of Baruch and Jabez: 1) God's collective program for his people supersedes personal comfort or ambition, 2) it's permissible to ask God to bless us during times of personal pain and 3) God in his sovereignty deals with each person's pain differently.

Jabez's prayer is not a magic formula that guarantees God's blessing if you repeat it every day. It does serve as an example of a real person who exercised faith, asked God to bless him and received his request. We must also remember that, "He [God] causes his sun to rise on the evil and the good, and sends rain on the righteous and the unrighteous" (Matthew 5:45). God is able to protect from the danger of the storm as well as bring blessing from it. He may use the same rain to preserve one crop while destroying another. The important question is, can I remain content in trusting him no matter how he answers my prayer, even when I cannot fully understand all that he is doing?

The contrast between Abraham and his nephew Lot is noteworthy. As their wealth grew, the size of their herds produced problematic overgrazing, which resulted in quarreling between their herdsmen, and Abraham took the initiative to maintain peace. He gave Lot first choice as they prepared to separate. Lot chose the best for himself. His "easy road" led him toward the materially comfortable but morally compromising life near Sodom (Genesis 13:11-13). Lot's name means "covering or tightly wrapped." He "covered himself" or we might say, "covered his bets" by choosing the best the world could offer. I'm sure he believed that this would result in his contentment. But by doing so he "tightly wrapped" himself and his family into a social system of moral decay that cost him dearly in the end. Lot clearly sought contentment through material gain but the New Testament tells us that his soul experienced "distress" and "torment" rather than peace (2 Peter 2:7-8).

Abraham, on the other hand, understood the risks of becoming enriched and obligated to the king of Sodom. In the account of Abraham going to battle to rescue Lot's family and the people of Sodom, he made it clear he would "accept nothing" for his military intervention, even going so far as to make an oath to the Lord declaring his steadfast intention to not receive any spoils of the battle (Genesis 14:22-24).

Gehazi, Elisha's servant, also was caught seeking contentment through possessions. After Elisha refused to take any payment from Naaman after he was healed from leprosy, Gehazi secretly hurried after him. Lying, he told Naaman that Elisha had changed his mind. He then took Naaman's well intentioned payment of silver and clothing for himself. He lied again when Elisha questioned him about his actions. Gehazi's name means "valley of vision" and it seems his vision had become clouded with coveting and filled with things. It is curious to note that even though he only took two talents of silver and two sets of clothing, Elisha questioned him, "Is this the time to take money, or to accept clothes, olive groves, vineyards, flocks, herds, or menservants and maidservants?" (2 Kings 5:26). It appears God was exposing the expansive vision of a greedy heart through these words of Elisha's prophecy. The price Gehazi paid for his actions stemming from his discontentment and covetousness was enormous. The words of God's judgment must have stung as their awful truth sunk in, "Naaman's leprosy will cling to you and your descendants forever" (v. 27).

Hezekiah is classified as one of the good kings of Judah. He came to the throne at age 25 and "did what was right in the eyes of the LORD" (2 Kings 18:3). "Hezekiah trusted in the LORD, the God of Israel. There was no one like him among all the kings of Judah, either before him or after him. He held fast to the LORD and did not cease to follow him" (vv. 5-6). Hezekiah's name means "God is my strength." When he was challenged by King Sennacherib of Assyria, he sought the Lord in a wonderful prayer acknowledging God's sovereign rule over all things. He pled for the people, and God answered powerfully. It is a great story of faith and God's faithfulness.

Hezekiah became ill at age 39 and hovered near death. The prophet Isaiah visited him and said, "This is what the LORD says; 'Put your house in order, because you are going to die; you will not recover'" (2 Kings 20:1). We are told that "Hezekiah turned his face to the wall…wept bitterly" (v. 2) and prayed. God responded by adding 15 years to his life. During those extra years of life two things occurred. First, he fathered Manasseh who later became one of the worst and most evil kings in the history of Judah. Second, he proudly displayed his wealth to envoys from Babylon. God revealed to him that as a result of that act, all his treasure would be carried off to Babylon along with his descendants. In his selfish response, he saw this as a good thing because the judgment would not fall during his own lifetime (v.19).

Hezekiah's story stands out as a reminder that it is possible to become self-focused and lose perspective in the second half of life, even after having finished an outstanding first half. Much discontentment in life can be traced back to the desire to live a little longer on this earth. It may be that his little story is included in the Scriptures to illustrate that sometimes God takes a person in death to spare them from evil

(Isaiah 57:1). Hezekiah was another curiously odd example from whom we can learn.

Jacob's story is well known. His name means "supplanter" or "one who takes the place of another." His life story was generally marked by trying to out maneuver others for personal gain. God was clearly at work in his life and graciously revealed himself to Jacob on several occasions. But Jacob was a slow learner and his discontentment level stayed high throughout most of the biblical narrative of his life.

When Jacob's wife Rachel was unable to have children "she said to Jacob, 'Give me children, or I'll die!'" (Genesis 30:1). He responded with anger. "Jacob became angry with her and said, 'Am I in the place of God, who has kept you from having children?'" (v. 2). The word "anger" can be translated "rage" and gives some idea of the level of discontentment between this husband and wife. Jacob's words were ironically revealing; he had been living in a manner that showed he had tried to supplant God's sovereign role in his life. Time and time again God placed Jacob into difficult situations to remind him that he was not sovereign over the events of his life.

It always leads to discontentment when anyone tries to be the sovereign lord of his or her life. Near the end of Jacob's life he was brought by his son Joseph before Pharaoh in Egypt. Jacob blessed him and then, "Pharaoh asked him, 'How old are you?'" (Genesis 47:9). What a wonderful opportunity for Jacob to be a missionary and give a vibrant testimony about the grace and power of God. But, instead he let his discontentment spill out of his heart when he said, "My years have been few and difficult" (v. 9). The word "difficult" can be translated "unpleasant." After all of God's protection and blessings, his perspective was still unhappy.

Jacob joins our group of curiously odd examples from whom we can learn. The Bible tells us that God loved Jacob (Romans 9:13) but Jacob was a slow learner who struggled with focusing his whole heart back on God, loving him and resting contently in God alone. Jacob's story gives me hope.

Reflection Questions and Small Group Activities:

1. With which of the curiously odd examples discussed can you most readily identify?

2. What other biblical examples teach lessons about contentment?

3. What examples of people outside the Bible provide lessons about contentment?

4. How can your small group continue to learn from each other about being content?

5. Ask the small group to write the highlights from their own stories about contentment and discontentment. Ask volunteers to share their stories with the group.

Prayer:

Thank you Father for providing the examples of real people for us to learn from. Help us to believe that you are just as interested in us as you were in the characters from the Bible. By faith help us learn contentment and believe that you can use our faith stories to touch others. Keep us faithful to the end. In Jesus' name we pray, Amen.

Chapter 11

Thanksgiving

*"Be joyful always; pray continually; give thanks
in all circumstances, for this is God's will for you
in Christ Jesus." 1 Thessalonians 5:16-18*

I remember spending a significant period of time with
a man who had difficulty saying the words, "thank you."
Once I noticed the absence of these familiar words from his
vocabulary, I became curious and began to pay more careful
attention thinking that I must not be hearing well or that
I was somehow mistaken in my observation. Maybe it was
an oversight or a temporary lapse of some kind. He was a
nice person, but the longer I listened and waited, the more
puzzled I became. Finally, I decided to do a little experiment
to see if I could elicit a "thank you." I decided to give him an
unexpected gift that was nice enough that it would naturally
call for an acknowledgment. It was a gift that I knew he
would genuinely appreciate. Then I waited. After some delay
we had a most painful and uncomfortable conversation. My
friend was very self-conscious and ill-at-ease. It was as if he
didn't know what to say or how to say it. It was very obvious
that I had put him in an awkward position. I will never know
why he had trouble saying the simple words, "thank you." He
did not disclose that to me and it was probably wrong of me
to put him through the discomfort of my little experiment.
When it was all over I regretted that my curiosity had
gotten the best of me and I felt saddened that it had been
so agonizing for him. It did, however, serve as a reminder
of how important it is to learn to freely speak the words of

thankfulness to others. Unfortunately, it is thanklessness that is on the rise.

I think of the story when Jesus healed the ten lepers and only one returned to express thanks (Luke 17:11-19). Jesus commended him for his faith, while drawing attention to the absence of the other nine. Expressing thanks is a common courtesy that we should practice to each other for the little things in life, and it is a significant issue in our spiritual development and relationship with God. Thanksgiving goes beyond sheepishly mouthing the words; it is a condition of gratefulness in the heart.

The Veggie Tales video *Madam Blueberry* got it right when one of the characters said, "A thankful heart is a happy heart."[8] We should all sit down and watch it with our children or grandchildren to remind us of this simple but important truth about thankfulness.

Today we read a newsletter from missionary friends serving in Swaziland. Their theme for the letter was thanksgiving. They wrote how often the Swazi people express thankfulness. "Siyabonga means thank you in siSwati. We hear it all the time—in Swazi prayers, in Swazi hymns, we hear it constantly in Swazi conversations. In fact, Swazis even express thanks just because you greet them. Siyabonga."[9]

8

Veggie Tales, Big Idea, Inc. 230 Franklin Road #2A, Franklin, TN 37064

9

Dudley and Inge Donaldson, Swaziland Express Newsletter. November 2009 – Vol. 2, Issue 11.

Contentment and thanksgiving go together. They are almost impossible to separate. I have observed that when discontentment wells up in a person's experience, thanksgiving dries up. The reverse is also true. When the giving of thanks stops, contentment becomes elusive. A spirit of entitlement cuts the heart out of thankfulness and is incompatible with a life of grace.

Lesson one: Contentment can be learned. God is at work and he is the master teacher.

Lesson two: Coveting is off limits.

Lesson three: God will provide.

Lesson four: Only God can truly satisfy.

Lesson five: Pursuing satisfaction in anything other than God is risky.

Lesson six: Learn to run.

Lesson seven: Give to those in need.

Lesson eight: Stop making comparisons.

Lesson nine: Realize that outwardly you are wasting away but inwardly you are being renewed.

Lesson ten: Learn from the example of others.

Lesson eleven: Give thanks.

Paul wrote, "Give thanks in all circumstances, for this is God's will for you in Christ Jesus" (1 Thessalonians 5:17). True thanksgiving guards us from a spirit of discontentment and reminds us that everything we are, and have, is a gift from God and is wrapped up in being in Christ (Ephesians 1:3,

2 Corinthians 8:9, James 1:17). It is God's will for us to see ourselves as being in Christ and blessed by God. It is in the everyday circumstances of life that we need to exercise faith in this truth. As we live out the implications of having been united with Christ, we will experience sweeter communion in prayer that is permeated with expressions of thanksgiving. This is the template of the Christian life that Paul returns to over and over again.

As one moves away from this model of grace for living, the more one will be weighed down with the burdens of life and will struggle to find contentment. Worship that is filled with consistent expressions of thanks and praise are part of the maintenance program for the contented heart.

[1]Come, let us sing for joy to the LORD; let us shout aloud to the Rock of our salvation.

[2]Let us come before him with thanksgiving and extol him with music and song.

[3]For the Lord is the great God, the great King above all gods.

[4]In his hand are the depths of the earth, and the mountain peaks belong to him.

[5]The sea is his, for he made it, and his hands formed the dry land.

[6]Come, let us kneel before the LORD our Maker; for he is our God and we are the people [7]of his pasture, the flock under his care. Psalm 95:1-7

Reflection Questions and Small Group Activities:

1. How do you cultivate thankfulness? Is it becoming a habit of your heart; a more frequent expression of your lips?

2. How have you noticed the connection between thankfulness and contentment in your life?

3. What types of circumstance make it difficult for you to express thanks?

4. To whom do you personally need to express your thanks?

5. Pretend it is Thanksgiving Day and you are sitting around the table. List your blessings and things for which you are thankful.

6. List the spiritual blessings for which you are most thankful.

7. Spend an extended time in prayer as a small group focusing on giving thanks.

Prayer:

Father, thank you for your love, grace and mercy expressed in the sacrifice of your Son, the Lord Jesus Christ, for our sins. Thank you for your gift of spiritual life in Christ and that all the spiritual blessings of heaven are found in him. Thank you for the promises you have made that are yet to unfold and that give us hope for the future. Teach us to be truly thankful people. In Jesus' name, amen.

Chapter 12

False Contentment and The Proper Role of Discontentment

"Blessed are those who hunger and thirst for righteousness, for they will be filled." Matthew 5:6

In an earlier chapter we examined a number of examples of people looking for contentment in the wrong places and in the wrong things. We have also observed that the pursuit of things other than God himself is dangerous because it enslaves, deadens the soul and robs us of true contentment. In drawing this discussion to a close, I need to underscore the obvious point that contentment is not generally found on the crowded freeway jostling for position in the fast lane of life. Learning godly contentment requires taking an occasional exit ramp and slowing down, so you can reflect on what is truly important. It may lead you to a less popular route. One must be ready to be misunderstood by friends, colleagues and even family. It may lead to a healthy discontentment with the status quo, and to a place of holy hunger that draws you to quietly feed your soul on the bread of life, to cultivate a yearning thirst that propels you to seek more of Christ, the water of life.

If you are serious about the pursuit of godly contentment, it will require some deliberate and strategic reorientation. You may not find much relief among the stampede of people committed to materialism or even much support from the crowd at the average success-oriented church. Lamentably most of Christendom looks pretty much like its surrounding culture. You will not only need to be alert to the dangers of pursuing the wrong goals but also must be alert to the spiritually deadening risks of false contentment.

What is false contentment? I believe that false contentment comes from believing that all is well when in reality it is not. It was the attitude of the religious leaders of Jesus' day. They showed a false contentment with the status quo. Another example of false contentment was that of the rich fool (Luke 12:16-21) who was satisfied in his own mind that the abundance he had stored was sufficient to provide much self-indulgent living. False contentment fails to realize that even though you are making progress toward the top, the ladder may be leaning against the wrong wall. False contentment forgets that life is brief, time is short and the danger of materialism is real. False contentment is filled with rationalizations that all is well.

If we are not focused on the realities of the heavenly kingdom we will fall into either a self-centered discontentment with our circumstances on one hand, or a sense of self-congratulatory false contentment on the other. If we blindly follow the crowd we will fall into one error or the other. Neither is good.

False contentment causes people to fall asleep spiritually. Paul tells us that the prevailing conditions upon the earth when Jesus returns will be characterized by spiritual slumber. "While people are saying, 'Peace and safety,' destruction will come on them suddenly" (1 Thessalonians 5:3). In other words, there will be widespread false contentment. He then goes on to warn of the importance to stay vigilant and awake (v. 6). Jesus also described the suddenness of his return and how he will interrupt while mankind is seeking after contentment in the normal activities of "eating and drinking, marrying and giving in marriage" (Matthew 24:36-41). It is easy to lose sight of eternal realities if we follow the crowd, seeking contentment through the celebrations that appear to give life its meaning. It was true in Noah's day and will continue until Jesus returns. The threat remains of being lulled to sleep, of living as if this is all there is, and forgetting that there is a greater reality soon to break in upon us. Jesus also asked, "However, when the Son of Man comes, will he find faith on the earth?" (Luke 18:8).

Contentment is found while seeking something else. It is serendipity. Jesus said, "Blessed are those who hunger and thirst for righteousness, for they shall be satisfied" (Matthew 5:6 NASB). Notice that righteousness is the object of the hunger and thirst, not contentment. Contentment is a byproduct of seeking the righteousness of Jesus.

This requires a discontentment with our own righteousness and a growing awareness of the unrighteousness around us. The prophet Ezekiel spoke about this kind of discontentment as grieving over the sin of his day when he recorded the message of the Lord, "Go throughout the city of Jerusalem and put a mark on the foreheads of those who grieve and lament over all the detestable things that are done in it" (Ezekiel 9:4). Proper discontentment should also mark the believer who is in tune with God's heart. It is that thread of ongoing repentance, the grief work of a heart that is broken over that which grieves the heart of God, that comes as we identify with the spiritual rebellion and moral decay around us. This is not pious finger pointing, but a true and genuine sadness that comes from walking with a righteous God in the midst of a fallen and broken world.

Only when a person comes to the realization that their personal righteousness is insufficient, does the gift of God's righteousness become precious. If you are content in your own righteousness you will not hunger for his righteousness. It is from this vantage point of desperate discontentment that a person will cry out in faith and repentance for the application of Jesus' righteousness. At the core of Paul's theology is the truth of becoming united with Jesus Christ (Romans 6:5) so that his life, death and righteousness can be applied to us. He also said that "this righteousness from God comes through faith in Jesus Christ to all who believe" (Romans 3:22). And, "God will credit righteousness – for us who believe in him" (Romans 4:24). Righteousness is therefore found in Jesus who is the source of true contentment. Only he can satisfy our hearts desire; not money, cars, houses, careers, accomplishments, leisure activities, sexual experiences, possessions, jobs, family, friends, food or drink. We were designed for nothing less than to be satisfied in God and God alone. He is the secret of true contentment.

Lesson one: Contentment can be learned. God is at work and he is the master teacher.

Lesson two: Coveting is off limits.

Lesson three: God will provide.

Lesson four: Only God can truly satisfy.

Lesson five: Pursuing satisfaction in anything other than God is risky.

Lesson six: Learn to run.

Lesson seven: Give to those in need.

Lesson eight: Stop making comparisons.

Lesson nine: Realize that outwardly you are wasting away but inwardly you are being renewed.

Lesson ten: Learn from the example of others.

Lesson eleven: Give thanks.

Lesson twelve: Contentment is a by-product of seeking the righteousness of Jesus.

Reflection Questions and Small Group Activities:

1. Why is it so easy to become distracted from ultimate spiritual realities by the normal celebrations of this life?

2. What practical steps can you take to keep eternity in view?

3. How can you pass on to your family a vibrant faith that will remain alert until Jesus comes?

4. Are you ready to take the road less traveled and possibly be misunderstood in order to seek genuine contentment?

5. Ask the members of your group to reflect back on which of the twelve lessons was most meaningful for them.

6. Ask for testimonies of practical steps that individuals have committed to take.

7. Pray for each other.

Prayer:

Lord, grant us a holy discontentment to understand that our smug, self-righteous accomplishments only lead to, and depend upon, false contentment. Give us a fresh taste of your grace to see and experience the realities of who you are, and all that you have done for us, in Christ. We cry out to you, Sovereign God, that you would give us a godly genuine discontentment with anything that leads us away from you. Let us taste the real contentment found in you that we can never achieve through our own effort, but which only comes from a deep work of your grace in our lives. We pray in Jesus' name, amen.